scm centrebooks

Christianity at the Centre/John Hick
Who is God?/D.W. D. Shaw
What about the Old Testament?/John Bowden
What is the New Testament?/T. G. A. Baker
What is the Church?/Victor de Waal
What is Right?/Michael Keeling
The Last Things Now/David L. Edwards
Who is Jesus Christ?/A. O. Dyson
What about the Children?/John Gray
Who is a Christian?/John Bowden
Why Pray?/Mark Gibbard
What is Man?/David Jenkins
Living with Guilt/Henry McKeating

Henry McKeating

Living with Guilt

SCM PRESS LTD

334 00911 1

First Published 1970
by SCM Press Ltd
56 Bloomsbury Street London WC1

© *SCM Press Ltd 1970*

Printed in Great Britain by
Billing & Sons Limited
Guildford and London

Contents

Foreword

I have really no business to be writing this book at all. I am not really a theologian, a fact which will be very obvious to anyone who is and who may happen to read this book. Any expertise I possess is in certain antiquarian studies related to the ancient Near East in general and the Old Testament in particular. My only excuse for writing is that the editor, for reasons best known to himself, asked me to do it.

As I write this book I am wearing two hats. There is my twentieth-century secular man's hat first of all. I can't help wearing it, because whether I like it or not I do live in the twentieth century and I share all the normal assumptions of my fellows. In spite of my job as a lecturer in a university department of theology and in spite of my right to the title 'Rev.', I do not find it any easier to believe in God than the next man. In fact I find it very difficult indeed.

But then there is my Christian believer's hat. I sometimes imagine I might be more comfortable without it, but I can't really get rid of that hat either. However hard it is to believe, I have so far found it quite impossible to stop believing altogether. So if there seems to be a certain ambiguity in my point of view, if I sometimes seem to write from the standpoint of an outsider, looking for a rational explanation of what Christians mean by guilt and of how the Christian idea of the atonement is supposed to work, and at other times sound like an insider, convinced and committed — if, I say, I give this impression, it is an entirely accurate one. Wearing my secular hat I find much traditional Christian language mystifying. I keep wanting to pin the words down, to keep asking what, in practical terms, they really mean. But with my believer's hat on I find that much of it makes sense, even when I can't explain it to myself very well. So I write in the hope of being just a little helpful to other people who feel as I do, who can see the reasons against being a Christian, but who also see some powerful difficulties in not being one.

I have tried for most of the book to wear my secular hat. I am convinced that, even if we leave God out of account, even if we reject some of the assumptions on which Christianity has been based, and much of the language in which it has been traditionally stated, there is still a great deal to be said for Christian insights into the nature of man, the nature of guilt and the necessity for atonement. I believe that there is much in the Christian view of these things which is valuable, even to secular man. I believe that there is much in them that is true, and which would remain true even if we had to decide that God does not exist. So for the first nine-tenths of the book I have tried to leave God out, and I have tried to see how far we can get without him. What remains is something less than the full Christian gospel, but it is not negligible. There is enough ground here to make it possible for Christian man and secular man to start talking to each other. But I want to make it clear that I do not myself want to stop at this point. Towards the end of the book I have asked myself the question, 'Granted that we can get so far without bringing God into it, how much further do we get when we do bring him in?' And this is where I have started to talk most like an insider and not an outsider.

Having said as much as I can say about Christianity in terms of my twentieth-century assumptions, I do not pretend that I have said all. I have to be prepared for the possiblity that at the end of the day some of my twentieth-century presuppositions will turn out to be wrong. And I have to allow that if the full richness of the gospel is to be appropriated, I must go back to the traditional statements and be prepared to understand them not in my terms but in theirs.

Many of the traditional statements about sin and guilt, and about atonement, strike us today as gruesome, risible or morally repulsive. But of all the grotesque, offensive, or otherwise

8

unhelpful expressions of the doctrine of the atonement there is none which Christians have not at some time felt valuable, and perhaps none that cannot in some moment 'click' with our own experience, so that we say, 'So *that's* what it's getting at'.

So if in this book I do not have a great deal to say about the traditional theories of the atonement, it is not because I am either ignorant of them or contemptuous of them. I am trying only to sketch some preliminaries to a theology of the atonement, to indicate one or two places at which modern man with modern prejudices may begin to understand what Christianity has been trying for all these years to say about guilt and its cure. I am not rejecting our traditional doctrines, only suggesting some points from which our traditional doctrines might be approached. However inadequate or objectionable some of the old explanations may at first sight appear to be, they are all worthy of respectful attention. Rabbi Ben Azzai said, 'Despise not any man, nor be contemptuous of any thing. For there is no thing which has not its place, and no man who has not his hour.'[1]

Thinking is a communal activity. The chances are, therefore, that if there are any useful ideas in this book they are other people's. I owe a good deal to discussions with my colleagues in the Theology Department of Nottingham University, a good deal to the house group of which I am a member, at Kingswood Methodist Church, Wollaton, and most of all to discussions with my wife, who I suspect could have written this book better than I have.

University of Nottingham,
Easter, 1970

NOTE

1. Mishnah, *Pirqe Aboth*, 4, 3.

1 Introduction

Most of us suffer from time to time from feelings of inadequacy. We are not on top of our job; or we feel ourselves to be inadequate parents, or inadequate lovers; or we just can't manage the housekeeping so as to make ends meet. And we feel at the same time that we *ought* to be able to do these things. If we can't it must be our own fault. We feel guilty.

Some of us suffer from feelings of guilt which we recognize, on reflection, to be irrational. We find ourselves feeling guilty about situations for which we cannot reasonably be blamed. But most of us know that there have been at least some occasions in our lives when we have been right to feel guilty. We have had something to feel guilty about.

Guilty feelings, even the irrational ones, cannot simply be wished away. If the occasion for them passes, we can forget, perhaps. But some of us are in situations from which we cannot escape, and in which we feel chronically inadequate, chronically guilty. As with most of the great human dilemmas, there is no question of finding a solution; the best we can do is to find some way of living with the problem.

I shall try in this book to explore, first, the sources of our feelings of inadequacy and guilt. Why do men have them at all? Why do they take the form they do in this generation? I shall then go on to look at some of the ways in which we try to deal with these feelings. As we go along I shall indicate ways in which it seems to me Christianity illuminates both the problem and the cure.

I shall try to do all this in as practical a way as possible, keeping to terms and ideas that seem to me to make at least a certain amount of sense in the twentieth century. It is my conviction that Christian insights into this question are valuable ones, and that they are still valuable even if one distrusts the traditional religious framework in which they have been developed and finds the religious language in which they have traditionally been expressed unhelpful.

Beginning from the common assumptions of twentieth-century western man, these insights can be stated in a way which is not totally unsatisfactory. And this is the way in which we *must* begin. If we Christians wish to explain our gospel to our contemporaries it is no good demanding that they learn our language first. We must show that, even accepting secular man's own presuppositions, some kind of explanation can be offered of how Christianity works, how it helps us to live with the dilemmas involved in being human.

I have avoided, I hope, technical theological terms and philosophical or quasi-philosophical language. I have done this not merely for the reader's sake, but for my own. If I am really to apprehend the Christian ideas about guilt and atonement, I must do it in words over which I do not stumble. I am not writing for a hypothetical man in the street or man in the pew who finds the language both of traditional religion and modern philosophy barely intelligible, and for whose imagination a personal deity remains stubbornly unreal: I am myself such a man.

It would appear at first sight that we cannot settle the question of atonement satisfactorily until we have settled the question of God. The traditional expositions of the atonement see sin as an offence against a personal individual God and the work of Christ as the satisfaction of God's honour, the averting of his wrath or the distracting on to himself of God's just punishment of sinners. To anyone who is not entirely convinced that God is personal, such presentations of the problem and its solution can have no interest at all. Can we any longer see our guilt in this light? Of course, some of us can, and do. Others of us believe that we ought to; but we don't feel it in our bones.

We therefore have to start at the other end, with the facts, or with the ideas that we do find convincing. People do have feelings of inadequacy and guilt. And they do believe that guilt can be something real; that there is such a thing as moral responsibility. This is common ground among all civilized and uncivilized men.

Very few men indeed would deny that guilt cannot be shrugged off. For the individual and for the society it creates problems. It has to be dealt with. How do we handle it and diminish the damage it can do?

Can we give the ideas of atonement and reconciliation a meaning that still stands up, even if we leave God out of the reckoning? Can we discover in the old language about sin and forgiveness, sacrifice and expiation, any usefulness or relevance? Can we salvage any image or idea that satisfies the mind and to which we can say, 'Yes, that helps. It lets me crystallize my dilemma and the dilemma of my society. It does something to my attitude towards my guilt. It shows me a direction in which I can do something positive about it'?

Whatever else may be said of them, the old stories and images did answer a human need, and for many of us still do. How and why do they do it? To what deeply felt convictions of the human mind are they giving voice?

The traditional Christian will immediately reply, 'But is this enough? Are they not more than stories or images? If we leave out the personal God, haven't we left out the thing that matters most?' Maybe we have. I do not pretend that the approach I have outlined does justice to the full Christian gospel as we have always stated it. But it is a beginning. Perhaps our conviction of the reality of God will come back, and the time will be ripe for a fuller statement.

But at the moment, even beginning from those few things of which, as secular men, we can be sure, we are not reduced to nothing. We may not be able, on this basis, to say with conviction all that the church has traditionally said about the atonement, but we are not reduced to silence.

The Christian in our time, like the ancient Jews after the sack of Jerusalem by the Romans, worships in a temple which has fallen about his ears, and from which even he admits the

13

Presence has departed. But he worships in hope of his temple's restoration and his God's return.

Even before we get around to talking about God, there is a great deal that we can say to this generation. We live in an age of intense moral awareness. Everything is presented as a moral issue and discussed in moral terms. And the preoccupation with morality is all the greater because we have abandoned religion and all other authority. We are possessed by the notion of human brotherhood, but having abandoned God, all we have left to blind us is compassion. We are also a disillusioned generation. We have lost faith in human capacity to succeed at the things that matter most. If the church has anything worth saying about guilt and expiation, this surely is not a time for silence, but neither is it a time for going on talking in a language our contemporaries do not understand.

2 What is Guilt?

Definitions

'Guilt' is an ambiguous word. It is used in two, or perhaps three, principal ways. First, it applies to *feelings* of guilt, whether rational or irrational. The psychologists habitually employ it in this sense. I have even heard a psychologist talk of a boy who 'had a guilt (*sic!*) about masturbation'. The psychologist, *qua* psychologist, is not usually interested in any other aspect of the matter. Guilt feelings are a phenomenon which it falls within his professional competence to do something about, but guilt in the other sense, guilt as a moral status, he will often dismiss as not within his province.

Nevertheless, most of us are convinced that it does make sense to use the word 'guilt' or 'guilty' in this second way, to indicate moral failure. And it is worth noting at this stage that there is no necessary connexion between feelings of guilt and the status of being guilty. It is possible to suffer from guilt feelings for which there is no rational justification, and for which even the sufferer himself knows there is no rational justification. It is also possible for a sufficiently hardened individual, or one well practised in self-justification, to do wrong and feel no guilt at all.

We ought probably to distinguish the legal meaning of 'guilt' from the moral meaning. One can certainly become morally guilty in a multitude of ways without transgressing the law. And we can no doubt all envisage circumstances in which the reverse might be true, in which a man might break the law and become technically guilty, but for good moral reasons. One can only deny this possibility by exalting respect for law into the supreme moral virtue.

15

In the rest of this book, however, I shall not be concerned with guilt as a legal status at all. I shall confine my discussions to the first two senses of the word and I shall try to distinguish very carefully between them. I shall say 'guilt feelings' when that is what I mean, and only use the word 'guilt' by itself when I am referring to the moral status. I shall try to be quite rigorous about this.

Guilt feelings: further analysis

Having made the distinction clear, let us examine guilt feelings more closely. What do these feelings consist in? It is difficult to be more precise than to say that they are feelings of discomfort which are not physical, or are not felt to be physical. A feeling of guilt is a feeling of having done something wrong, and cannot be analysed away into anything else. Guilt feelings may be aroused by a number of different causes; they may differ in intensity but do not differ in kind according to the causes arousing them.

I get an uncomfortable feeling, let us say, if I walk under a ladder. If the bus conductor overlooks me when collecting the fares and I do not call attention to myself I also get an uncomfortable feeling. Are they the same feeling? Reason tells me that I ought to laugh at myself for paying attention to the first and be ashamed of myself for ignoring the second. But this is not a means of discriminating between the feelings themselves; it is reason's judgment on the phenomena that prompted them. It seems to me that the feelings themselves are indistinguishable.

Why do I get these feelings at all? Why should either of these sets of circumstances give rise to them? I suppose that in both of these particular instances the answer lies in my childhood experiences. I was brought up by a mother who always asserted most strenuously that she was not superstitious; but crossed knives, or shoes on the table horrified her. Her horror, no doubt, communicated itself to my impressionable young mind, ineradicably. I was also brought up by a mother who instilled into her children a quite Victorian rectitude. Her horror of dishonesty (reinforced by that of all my other God-fearing relatives, teachers and friends) communicated itself to me also. It would appear, then, that my uncomfortable feelings take their rise initially from other people's approval and disapproval. In the one case they are weakened by rational reflection, and in the other strengthened by a multitude of factors.

I do not think that all guilt feelings arise from this single root, i.e. from other people's disapproval. I shall have more to say about this in a minute. I want first to make some other observations.

My example demonstrates that the uncomfortable feelings are not under the rational mind's control. Reason may lead me to disregard the feeling about the ladder, but it does not stop me experiencing it.

Moreover, if guilt feelings are much the same, whether they arise from rational or irrational causes, and if the rational mind cannot get rid of them, then irrational feelings of guilt can cause just as much trouble in the *psyche* as rational ones.

We may note in passing that though we ourselves can usually appreciate when our guilt feelings arise from some moral cause and when they do not, ancient man frequently failed to make the distinction. He tended to treat the uncomfortable feelings exactly alike, whatever their source, and to give them all equal weight. If he walked over a grave it worried him in the same way as if he had misappropriated his neighbour's goods, and he resorted to much the same kind of procedure for dealing with his worry. This is a fact we have to bear in mind when evaluating ancient religious rites.

The biological roots of guilt feelings

Biologically speaking, man is an animal. Like all animals, he has strong instincts of self-preservation. But he is also a social animal. Social animals have another set of instincts, ones which dispose them to defend and care for other members of their species, or at least of their herd. Solitary animals survive best if their instincts for self-preservation are strong. Social animals survive best if the individuals' instincts for self-preservation can be overridden by the desire to protect the group. To put it in evolutionary terms, there was a biological advantage in favour of the species whose members were prepared, when self-interest and the interests of group were in conflict, to submerge self-interest for the sake of their fellows.

For thousands of generations, therefore, man has had strengthened in him by the process of evolution a device which causes serious conflict in his inmost being. The evolutionary process has provided him with powerful instincts for self-preservation, which translate themselves into urges to satisfy his individual appetites for food, sex and power, and at the same time with a built-in conviction that he ought to control those urges, and even, at times, to sacrifice his self-interest to that of his fellow men.

In these basic biological facts lies the root of the dreadful tension between 'I want' and 'I ought'. This tension has, as it were, been programmed into the biological machine which we call man. Given the strength of his self-directed instincts it is inevitable that he often allows them to take precedence. 'I ought' gives way to 'I want'. But when this happens, man gets an acutely uncomfortable feeling, the biological function of which is to encourage him to give precedence to 'ought' over 'want'; to put the group's interests above his own. The psychologist calls the uncomfortable feelings 'feelings of guilt'. The moralist may call them 'pangs of conscience'.

There is more to the matter than this. For the 'other-directed' instincts of the social animal include among them a strong tendency to seek the group's approval and avoid its disapproval. When the individual allows self-interest to come first he incurs the group's disapproval. When he puts the group's interest first he enjoys its approval. So he not only has what we might call an 'altruistic' tendency built into him, but also a secondary mechanism by which that tendency is repeatedly strengthened.

The uncomfortable feelings act as a watchdog over the individual on the group's behalf. If the individual does what the group disapproves of, the feelings arise whether the group is there to see or not.

The uncomfortable feelings form what we might call the

raw conscience, the basis of conscience. There is a thinking conscience which sometimes challenges and may set aside the promptings of the raw conscience. In modern society no individual belongs solely to one, closely knit social group. He belongs to a number of such groups, and is aquainted with many more. Different groups approve and disapprove of different things. The raw conscience of the small child is directed by the approval and disapproval of his parents and family, but as soon as he goes to school he may find himself called on to adopt different behaviour patterns. The society of his contemporaries playing in the street may thrust upon him different patterns again. To some extent he solves the difficulty by evolving different behaviour patterns for each context, but some rudimentary reflection is necessary even at this stage.

The maturing man, moving from one social group to another, not only finds reflection forced upon him, obliging him to make explicit choices between the approval of this group or that, but may well find the raw conscience out of step with his reflective judgment. If I am brought up in the bosom of a religious sect, for whom it is sinful to drink, smoke, swear, gamble, or go to theatres or cinemas, I may well decide, on reflection, that some of these are innocent pastimes and that I need not have a bad conscience about indulging in them. But if I do indulge in them I may experience the old uncomfortable feelings none the less. It is a long time before the ex-teetotaller can walk into a pub without feeling sheepish, or at least defiant.

We conclude that though the conscience begins in our inbuilt desire to serve the interests of our fellows, and in our desire for their approval, it does not consist merely in this. It contains a reflective element. Furthermore, if this were all, the individual could never feel impelled by his conscience to defy the society of which he is a member. The fact that this phenomenon does occur would seem to be a serious objection to the explanation of conscience which I have developed so far. I think, however, that objection can be met at least in part.

In the first place, the individual could feel that in defying his social group and incurring its disapproval, he was acting in their own interests. The Hebrew prophets criticized the behaviour of their contemporaries, incurring heavy disapproval in the process. But they believed that if their fellow Israelites continued to behave as they were doing, disaster would overtake the country. The criticism was therefore in their fellow countrymen's own real interests. (This was not, of course, the prophets' only motive, by any means.)

Further, the moralist who condemns his own society sees himself, in a very large number of instances, not as a revolutionary but as a reactionary. He may look like an innovator, but in his own eyes he is often recalling his society to older and better ways. He is appealing to standards which, perhaps in an earlier generation, that same society laid down. Or (and this is another form of the same phenomenon) he may be appealing to principles which the society already in theory subscribes to. The critic, in this case, is claiming to be truer to his society's own principles than the society itself. He is, as it were, looking beyond the judgment of his immediate contemporaries to that of some ideal form of the community, represented perhaps by the founding fathers or by posterity. The Hebrew prophets again illustrate the point, for they certainly believed that they were recalling their people to ancient ways, and to the conditions of that covenant with God in which the people themselves claimed to stand.

There is yet another way in which an individual may feel compelled by his conscience to defy his society. What he may in fact be doing is re-defining the society to which he owes allegiance. I shall have more to say about this idea later, but here let me offer one example to make clear what I mean. Among the cotton plantations of the USA before the civil war a man could badly mistreat his black slave without incurring the disapproval of his white friends. He was sensitive to the approval and disapproval of his white fellows, but his conscience had never been educated to respond in the same way to the black ones. As far as his raw conscience was concerned, 'society' meant 'white society'. The abolition of slavery was in a sense a call to redefine society so as to include black men as well as white, and so that a man would feel the same responsibility towards his fellow, of whatever colour.

I do not assert that the biological explanation of guilt feelings and of conscience is entirely adequate to explain all the phenomena concerned. I only maintain that we can explain a good deal about guilt feelings and the conscience without resort to the traditional 'mystic' theories, and indeed, that we can explain some things better on the basis of the view I have advanced than on that of the traditional theories. If the conscience is some sort of divinely implanted faculty giving us knowledge of right and wrong, why is it that the consciences of good and godly men so often disagree? 'An erring conscience,' said Kant, 'is a chimaera.' On the contrary, it is a depressingly familiar phenomenon.

Guilt feelings, I conclude from all this, are inseparable from the nature of man. They arise out of the tension between his self-directed and his other-directed propensities. Often they are useful. Sometimes they are an embarrassment, especially when they become displaced and are aroused by behaviour which the reasoning mind does not condemn. There are plenty of factors at work in the modern world exacerbating our feelings of guilt. We shall now examine some of these.

The exacerbating factors

Man is an organism with an unparalleled capacity for changing his environment. But many of the changes which he makes have results which he does not foresee. The larger the scale of his activities, the more difficult it is for him to predict the economic, social and ecological consequences of what he does. Consequently, although he is constantly striving to make his environment more comfortable and convenient for himself, he often solves one problem only at the cost of creating others.

Man also has unrivalled powers of adaptation, but he is now changing his environment at such a pace that he tends to outstrip these powers. New problems, new situations keep arising. We barely have time to adjust ourselves to them before the next round of changes is on its way. Not only individuals, but society

21

as a whole, its institutions and its social machinery, feel the strain. This is a great source of tension, of feelings of inadequacy, and hence the guilt.

Quite apart from the problems attendant on the rapid pace of change, there is another, inherent in civilization itself. Man inherits instincts and urges which were doubtless valuable to the species when they first evolved but which are sometimes, in our man-made environment, very embarrassing. These more violent instincts have to be controlled for most of the time. Controlling them again gives rise to tension. They may be exercised in imagination, but this itself often creates feelings of guilt. They can only be legitimately exercised when society finds use for them in specialized situations, such as war, or makes artificial outlets for them, as in sport.

The aggressive urges may also be channelled into other kinds of competitiveness. Occasionally they may prompt individuals to pursue with energy socially useful ends, but just as often the result is socially harmful. People who give their competitive and aggresive instincts free rein when driving their cars may be getting rid of embarrassing instinctual energy, but hardly in a socially useful way.

The evolutionary process frequently encumbers the developing organism with left-overs, which continue to be reproduced when they are no longer useful. If the environment changes faster than the organism can adapt itself, the organism may die out. It is too much encumbered with the attributes which enabled it successfully to fight the last war but one, but which prevent it from efficiently fighting the present one.

Anatomically, man has a number of such vestiges. He has an appendix, which was presumably useful to his ancestors, but which only exposes him to the risk of appendicitis. Evolution has not got rid of the human appendix. However, man himself has invented surgical techniques which enable him to do just that, in cases where the appendix might kill him.

The appendix was made redundant by changes in man's feeding habits which took place millions of years ago, but more recent changes have placed even greater strain on the capacities with which nature endowed him. Man has an eyeball and a visual system which stand up badly to the demands which he now makes on them. He is obliged to invent spectacles, mechanically adapting his eye to the environment, as nature has so far failed to do biologically.

Man has a brain and nervous system so designed that when travelling at his natural speed (maximum about 20 mph), his speed of reaction is amply quick enough. He drives motor cars and other surface vehicles at speeds well in excess of his natural 20 mph and thereby puts considerable strain on his natural capacities. The suprising thing is not that he sometimes has accidents but that he manages for so much of the time not to.

In such ways does the environment which man himself has shaped make demands on him. He pushes his natural capabilities to their limits. This is easy to see in the case of his physical capacities. It may be less obvious, but is equally true, of his mental ones.

Man not only has redundant organs, like the appendix, but he has created an environment in which some of his instincts are largely redundant too. In an over-populated world he is encumbered with sexual urges far stronger than his race needs. In a civilized world he has combative instincts which are embarrassingly well-developed. He has as yet invented few mechanisms which adapt his *psyche* as well as spectacles adapt his eye. He has made a beginning with drugs. He can, with drugs, relieve his tensions when the strain becomes severe. He can use them, not to control his sexual urges (this would doubtless be possible, but unacceptable) but to control their results by suppressing or depressing his fertility. But drugs, so far, are a very crude instrument.

The strains which man imposes on himself, and his resulting difficulty in coping with the complexities of his own world, inevitably lead to feelings of inadequacy and feelings of guilt.

Much of man's tension is associated with growth in the size of the community to which he belongs. As long as mankind was organized in small, discrete communities there was scope for man's altruistic instincts inside the community and for his

23

aggressive instincts outside it, in conflict with other communities. But it is no longer easy for the individual to define the community to which he belongs. We have doubts about what the social unit is which claims our first loyalty. I have said that the job of conscience is to encourage the individual to put his people before himself. Primitive man knew who his people were. They were his family or tribe. Feudal man knew that his first loyalty was to his lord or to his city. For the last two or three centuries most of us in the west have known that our first loyalty was to our nation. Obviously there was always some scope for conflict, but never so much as now. Now patriotism is in decline. The feeling is growing that our first allegiance should be not to our country but to humanity. If anyone doubts this, let him reflect that many of the expressions of patriotism which a generation or two generations ago were regarded as acceptable, or even fine – 'My country, right or wrong', for example – are regarded as almost obscenely immoral by most of the young. Some find it nearly incredible that anyone should ever have expressed such sentiments.

At present we find ourselves in a fluid situation. We have not entirely abandoned the old national loyalties, neither have the new and wider ones yet won the day. This uncertainty about the nature of the community to which we owe first allegiance is one of the factors creating moral confusion, because a shift of perspective here has far-reaching moral consequences.

A very clear illustration of this is found in Arthur Miller's play, *All My Sons*.[1] I shall have occasion to refer to this work again, so I shall outline the story fully at this point. The action is set in America during the last war. The principle character, Joe Keller, is a manufacturer of aero-engines. He has knowingly allowed defective engines to leave the factory, with the result that men have been killed. Joe has been charged with the crime and has cleverly managed to shift the blame on to his partner. However, no one has many doubts about his real responsibility. Joe himself has no conscience about what he has done. He does not feel guilty; he feels smart.

Joe's son is an airman, and is missing. At the climax of the play a letter is revealed, written by the missing son. He has heard of his father's trial. He has gone on a flying mission with the deliberate intention of not coming back. It is this which breaks through to Joe's reluctant conscience.

Joe at first did not feel guilty because he did not question that his loyalty to his family was paramount. He only sees the significance of what he has done when someone shows him that he ought to feel loyalty to those beyond the family. Only the revelation that he is responsible for his own son's death convinces him that they were all, all his sons.

This illustrates the consequences of the change in perspective for an individual. But our whole society is in the process of changing its perspective in this way. White men and black men have existed side by side for centuries, but only now do we have a colour *problem*. We only recognize the problem because we are enlarging our idea of community, and have begun to believe that we have an obligation to all other human beings. We have enlarged the definition of 'my people'. The defendants at the Nuremberg trials were mostly accused of 'crimes against humanity'. This is a striking phrase. And the clear principle established during those trials, that there are circumstances in which duty to humanity overrides the normal imperatives of military discipline and of patriotism in war, marks an enormous change in the moral assumptions of mankind.

But the change is far from complete. At present we are uncertain where our loyalties ought to lie. In some contexts our country seems to make the first claim, in some our family, and in some the human race. Others of us may, at least in some situations, feel strong loyalties to our city, or to our class. If there were a clear hierarchy of loyalties, this would not matter, but there is none. The result is conflict, uncertainty, and feelings of guilt.

There are other ways in which the circumstances of modern life increase moral uncertainty, and some of them are almost too obvious to need mention. Our increasing technical expertise opens up new possibilities which raise moral problems of their own. These are new problems. They have never arisen before

25

and therefore there are no existing guidelines. Organ transplants, artificial insemination and contraception are examples that spring immediately to mind. The first two of these directly affect few people, though the problems they raise for society are very acute. The last example affects nearly all of us directly. It can be foreseen that the use of computers will in the near future raise serious problems, too, and these may be harder to solve, for whereas on the issue of contraceptives we can agree to differ, and each individual (or couple) act as conscience dictates, on the large-scale use of computers we shall have to agree.

Can moral rules change?

There is one very large question which causes moral confusion. The world is changing. Society is changing. But we constantly face the new conditions with attitudes and values formed when things were different. Consequently there is often a clash between the demands of common sense and the demands of our inherited traditional values or moral rules. This clash is all the sharper because many of us are convinced that moral values are immutable.

Let us look at some examples of the way in which changing social conditions and changing technical possibilities call existing moral values in question. I shall spend a little time on this, as some readers may need a good deal of convincing.

The human characteristics that a society values most are the ones that are of most use to it at the time. A society whose economy is based on hunting or which is frequently engaged in war will put courage at the top of its list of virtues. A settled society will lay more weight on the less aggressive aspects of the human character, i.e. it will have a different scale of moral values. When certain European countries were liberated from Nazi control during the war some 'freedom fighters' became bandits virtually overnight. They had not changed their style of life at all, but society had changed radically. The qualities in which these men excelled were of great value to their countries under enemy occupation, but a positive embarrassment under

26

conditions of independence. Changes in society are bound to change the hierarchy of moral values, though not usually in such dramatic ways.

Throughout most of history human beings have had to work virtually all their available time in order to meet their basic requirements for food, warmth, etc. Hard work has therefore always been a prime virtue, and idleness one of the most serious sins. Of course, there have always been particular groups *within* society as a whole, such as the aristocracy, who did not need to work to keep body and soul together. Within such groups idleness was no disgrace, and other virtues, such as chivalry, took precedence over hard work.

We have long entered the phase in which society no longer needs all the work its members are capable of doing. It therefore limits the amount they do, by discouraging them from working before they are sixteen or after they are sixty-five; by persuading them that they are entitled to two days' rest a week and three weeks' holiday a year, and that if they work forty hours in any week they deserve to spend the rest in idleness.

We have adjusted our practice to our needs, but have not completely adjusted our thinking. We still assume that hard work is in itself a virtue, and cannot admit to ourselves that in the present conditions of western society this is no longer so. Our annoyance with the hippies is largely due to the fact that they have noticed this and act accordingly. We are obliged to find ways of justifying the extra work we do, so we invent a new goal, that of raising our standard of living. And we often talk (or our politicians do) as if raising the standard of living were itself a moral obligation. Or we justify it by competitiveness. We cannot pretend that *society* needs all our labours, so we assert that they are necessary to us as individuals in order to enable us to 'get on', that is, to get ahead of the next chap. But individual competitiveness is itself quickly becoming a redundant virtue, though in some ways our social system stimulates it more and more.[2]

Honest recognition of such facts as these would immediately relieve many of us of a good deal of anxiety and feelings of guilt. Why does the housewife with her home full of labour-saving machinery feel a compulsion to be *busy* all the time, neutralizing the advantage of her labour-saving gadgets by setting herself ever higher standards of cleanliness and smartness? She is driven onwards by an outdated ethic, which tells her that the time she saves in not ironing the non-iron shirts and in not darning the nylon socks and in not washing the throw-away underwear must be spent in *something*, if only in washing the washable wallpaper – a job which her grandmother, for excellent reasons, never felt obliged to do.

Our needs change. Common sense demands that we adjust our behaviour, but we do not adjust our moral values. So a tension is set up between the obvious demands of common sense and the demands of our our-of-date ethic. Guilt feelings are the result.

What we have to acknowledge is that ethical rules must change as the conditions under which society operates change, and there is a general reluctance, not only amongst religious people, to allow that ethical rules can change at all. Nowhere is this issue more keenly contested than in the field of sexual ethics.

An act must be judged moral or immoral according to its predictable or possible consequences. If for some reason the likely consequences change, or if the conditions of society so change that the same consequences become more desirable, or less so, then the moral status of the act must be evaluated afresh.

Let us apply these principles to the act of extra-marital sexual intercourse. One important reason, though not the only one, why such acts have traditionally been condemned is that there was always a possiblity of unwanted pregnancy. For this reason it was always an irresponsible act. The use of oral contraceptives removes this possibility, reliably. This does not mean that we can now assert that pre-marital or extra-marital sexual intercourse is morally innocuous. There are probably still good reasons for condemning it. What can be said, most emphatically, is that we cannot continue to discuss the matter *as if nothing had changed*, or pretend that the moral issues are what they have always been.

I am aware that traditional Christian ethics would challenge my initial premise, that the moral status of an act depends on its consequences. Many Christians would say that extra-marital sexual intercourse is wrong *in itself*. But the traditional rule: outside marriage – wrong!, inside marriage – right!, though simple and clear-cut, has always clouded the issue in two major respects. It has suggested that all extra-marital intercourse is *equally* wrong. It has looked on the one hand at the young man, genuinely in love, engaged to be married, and carried away by the strength of his feelings; and on the other hand at the married man who resorts to prostitutes or goes off for a dirty weekend with his secretary; *and has regarded them as guilty of the same sin*. Traditional morality has stuck on both of them the same label, 'fornification', and treated them as equal. Common sense rightly rebels. Doubtless the young man carried away by his feelings is wrong, but he is a lot less wrong than the other.

One result of this is that traditional morality has lost a great deal of respect, but this is not what concerns us at the moment. It is another example of how traditional ethical attitudes can get out of step with what one mght call 'common sense ethics'. And this gives rise to unnecessary guilt feelings, or guilt feelings on an unnecessary scale.

The other respect in which the traditional clear-cut rule has clouded the issue, and I mention this only in parenthesis, is that it has encouraged the assumption that within marriage sexual intercourse is always right. But the possibility of unwanted pregnancy can be a *moral* reason for refraining from intercourse within marriage. And the husband who disregards his wife's fears and insists on his 'rights' commits an act as crassly immoral as fornification.

The examples mentioned could be multiplied. In very many respects our moral assumptions are out of line with the morality our society requires. It is not surprising that in this situation we suffer from feelings of guilt which are hard to resolve. In the long run, when traditional morality and common sense conflict, common sense wins, but in the short run it can cause a vast amount of misery.

Changes in our understanding of human behaviour

Having looked more closely at feelings of guilt and at some of the ways in which present-day conditions make them worse, let us now look at the notion of moral responsibility itself. We now understand a good many things about human behaviour which former generations did not understand, and this has made a difference to the way in which we apportion blame.

Psychology and sociology between them have taught us three major truths about human behaviour. They have taught us how much an individual's behaviour may be at the mercy of his own inherited mental constitution; how much at the mercy of his own earlier, formative experiences; and how much it may be affected by the society to which he belongs, the values it has imparted to him and the expectations it may have of him. These are commonplaces and it is perhaps unnecessary to enlarge upon them.

All these insights affect the way in which we attach blame. While it is still going too far to say that 'tout comprende est tout pardonner', it is nevertheless true that the more we understand of the reasons for someone's anti-social behaviour the less we are generally inclined to blame him.

But few of us could be brought to admit that the notion of blame has become meaningless. We may appreciate that little Johnny who is a delinquent was brought up in a slum, that he went to a slum school, that his parents were divorced and that in any case he is of very low intelligence, and all this will certainly make us inclined to blame him *less*, but does it mean that we cannot blame him *at all*? Is there not another factor in the situation which is under Johnny's own control? Why is Johnny's brother, who was brought up in the same conditions and is just as unintelligent, a responsible and industrious citizen, against all the odds?

There is an introspective argument that carries even more weight than this. No one can be brought to admit that his own actions are entirely predetermined, either by his inherited make-up or his environment. We may have a quite acute appreciation of our own weaknesses, and may recognize that some of them are weaknesses we were born with, and that others are the result of the way in which we were brought up, but we still cannot get rid of the conviction that we ought to be able to overcome them, and that we are blameworthy if we do not at least make the attempt.

In practice it is almost always futile to try to assess moral responsibility in individual cases. It is easy enough to distinguish the two ends of the spectrum, between premeditated wrong-doing, undertaken for profit, and compulsive behaviour which is the product of mental aberration; between the great train robbers, for example, and the kind of kleptomaniac who steals nothing but green mackintoshes. But the vast majority of crime and of other reprehensible behaviour does not fall clearly into either category. It is a well-established fact that a very high proportion of convicted criminals, and an especially high proportion of habitual ones, show more or less clear signs of mental disorder. And it is generally acknowledged that many criminals are not motivated primarily by a desire for gain. Many thefts are committed by people who do not really want what they have stolen; who simply give it away or abandon it. Crimes are committed by people who take no trouble to avoid detection or capture. Much crime, in short, proceeds not from premeditated wickedness but from inadequately controlled and imperfectly expressed needs and urges of other kinds. And there is little doubt that, even where motives of profit predominate, the other components are often not entirely lacking. This is especially true of the more violent crimes, until when we come to the most violent crime of all, murder, the proportion committed in a premeditated way, for profit, is extremely small.

What applies to overt crime applies to anti-social behaviour of most other sorts. It is the result of forces within our own nature which are only imperfectly under our control. When other people behave badly we are ready to see them as entirely culpable. When we ourselves behave badly we realize how much of it is due to forces and tensions within us which are sometimes too much for us. I make a nasty remark to my wife (let us say);

I apologize, but somehow, entirely contrary of course to my intentions, the apology ends in a flaming row. Why? I may not fully understand myself how it happened. The tensions within me led to behaviour of which I myself disapprove; and disapprove not only in retrospect, but while I am actually indulging in it. Could I have helped it? Nothing will shake my conviction that I *ought* to have helped it. It is equally certain that that same conviction will not stop it happening again.

Thus, when we behave badly we *feel* as if we are morally responsible. We feel guilty. And the rational mind frequently confirms that we are right to do so. We *are* morally responsible, and yet in very many instances we are not totally responsible. We are in part at the mercy of forces within us which we cannot entirely control.

Not all wrongdoing, of course, arises in the way described. We may act wrongly, not because our emotions are too strong or our tempers too quick but through a kind of failure of imagination. We do not appreciate what it feels like to be on the receiving end, or how the other people involved will react; or we are not able to visualize vividly enough the consequences of what we do or how we shall feel about it afterwards. Wickedness, like courage, often proceeds from a circumscribed imagination. How far we can be held responsible for shortcomings such as these it is impossible to say.

In other instances our conscience itself may not be very sensitive to the wrong in question. Consciences have to be educated. They are educated largely by our fellows. And if the education has been lacking, then we shall have defective consciences. I once heard a Frenchman speak of his upbringing in Algeria under the colonial régime. He was aware, he said, that Algerian peasants lived in a very different style from the *colons*; that they were, by European standards, desperately poor, piteously housed, and often undernourished. He did not see this as a problem. He assumed that Algerian peasants were 'different'. They were used to such conditions, therefore they didn't mind them. It was only as an adult that it struck him with the force of a revelation that these people had the same needs and feelings as himself. No one had ever shown him this. His conscience had never been made aware of it.

How far is the individual in such circumstances responsible for his own moral blindness? Clearly he is not *altogether* responsible. Equally clearly he does not altogether *lack* responsibility. Wherever we turn, we are forced to the same conclusion.

It might seem reasonable to say that a man cannot be held responsible for the urges and forces within him, but only for the way in which he controls or fails to control those urges. The child can't help coveting the trinkets that lie exposed so near to hand on Woolworth's counter; the man can't help fancying the pretty girl sitting opposite in the tube. But provided they are not actually psychotic, the child is not obliged to commit theft or the man to attempt seduction.

But we have seen that this simple distinction will not work. The man's capacity to resist the temptation or the child's appreciation of the wrongness of the act may themselves be compromised by factors for which they are not wholly responsible. For example, the child may have parents who themselves treat pilfering lightly, and never ask questions about anything he brings home.

There is thus no easy way out of the dilemma. We have ample evidence that human beings, including ourselves, are not entirely responsible for their actions. Yet we cannot rid ourselves of the conviction that they are responsible to a degree.

Corporate responsibility

We have seen, then, how the insights of psychology and sociology make it harder for us to pin total blame on individuals for what they do. It is noteworthy, however, that in some instances we are only able to diminish the blame we attach to individuals at the cost of transferring it elsewhere, on to society.

If we are not to blame little Johnny too much for being a delinquent, on the grounds that he grew up in circumstances which made it difficult for him to be anything else, we cannot help asking who was responsible for those circumstances. Why didn't Johnny's parents look after him better? Or were they as much a prey to their environment as he? Who allowed the slum houses and the slum schools to exist? We only have to ask such questions to appreciate that behind the corrupt Johnny stands a corrupt society. Johnny just happens to be one of the points where the corruption shows.

If a man has an uneducated conscience and it isn't entirely his fault, who are the educators? Of course, some people make it their special task, either as professionals or as amateurs, to sharpen the moral awareness of the rest of us: the long-haired protesters, the cassandras of the popular press, the television interviewers are all engaged largely in moral education. But though they make it their special job they are no more responsible for it than the rest of us. In the field of morals all are the educators of all.

It is worth while spending a little time on this notion of communal responsibility, because it is one which has raised considerable difficulty in the past. It has sometimes been argued that corporate responsibility or corporate guilt do not make sense. It is individuals who are morally responsible, not groups. Now I do not pretend that there are no difficulties in the idea, but it does seem to me that there are fewer difficulties in it than there appeared to be a generation or two generations ago. We no longer think in such rigidly individualistic terms as we once did. We are aware that 'the individual man' is in some sense a philosophic abstraction. Real men exist only in societies. And if they did not grow up amongst and learn from their fellows they would not recognizably be 'men' at all. It may well be that in a few decades it will be the notion of *individual* responsibility that people will find it difficult to make sense of.

Certainly a sense of social solidarity is something that is universal. I am watching an England versus Ireland match on the telly on Saturday afternoon. My small daughter wanders through the room. 'Is that football?' 'No, rugby.' 'Who's playing?' 'England and Ireland.' 'Are we winning?'

What makes her say 'we'? It is nothing she has caught from me. I enjoy rugby, but in a very non-partisan way. What deep solidarity does my small daughter feel with those fifteen large,

34

muddy gentlemen that she so casually refers to them as 'we'? She evidently feels the same solidarity with the dead, for she is equally capable of asking. 'Did we win the battle of Waterloo?'

At the popular level I do not think that this idea has ever caused difficulty. The difficulty would be to get along without it. We do feel that members of a community belong together in such a way that the action of one is the action of all. Why else should any of us be pleased when a British athlete wins an Olympic medal or a British football team a world cup?

And this is not only a manner of speaking or a question of sentiment. Government would be impossible without this sense of solidarity, and without acceptance of the fact that the action of one can bind all. The decision of a British cabinet minister is treated as a decision of 'the cabinet' or 'the government'. From abroad it will be regarded as a decision of 'The United Kingdom'. It will reflect credit or discredit on all these corporate bodies, and its consequences may well involve every inhabitant of these islands. Within the country the minister's decision will be seen not only as a decision of the government but as the decision of a party; as a socialist decision or a conservative one. And the party too will gain or lose by it.

The idea of corporate responsibility has practical consequences not only in government but in law. What do we make of the fact that an injured miner may sue the National Coal Board for negligence? From the point of view of a philosopher, the attribution of negligence to so nebulous a body as the Coal Board may seem faintly ridiculous, but it is no laughing matter for the miner if he stands to gain £10,000 or so.

Life as we know it could not go on if corporate bodies could not be held responsible for their actions or the actions of their members. We do often talk as if moral responsibility could be attached to communities. Statements like, 'The Germans were to blame for the Second World War', or, 'The colonial powers have a lot to answer for', are felt by most of us to be meaningful. (Whether we agree with them or not, we should all admit that they make enough sense to be worth arguing about.)

I may have laboured the point about corporate responsibility, but it is important to establish it. For a long time we have been told that traditional Christian statements about sin and guilt and atonement were unhelpful because they are framed in terms of corporate and communal concepts which modern western men cannot understand. Whatever justification there may have been for these arguments in recent decades, I suggest that there is none now.

What is happening, indeed, is that our ideas of corporate personality are expanding. We are conscious today not only of our identity as Liverpudlians (citizens of no mean city) or Cornishmen or Britons, but as members of the human race. The phrase 'the human race' is itself a highly significant one, and the frequency with which we use it nowadays is more significant still. It points to a solidarity which we feel with other human beings of all sorts or any sort. This is probably a new phenomenon in history; it is new, at any rate, in its scale.

The attitude to the moon landings is indicative of the general feeling. They are, of course, an American achievement and would probably never have happened at all except for the spirit of rivalry that exists between America and the Soviet Union (to say nothing of the military reasons for developing rocketry). But they are also being presented as an achievement of humanity as a whole, as 'a big step forward for mankind'.

Thus, on a world-wide scale we are prepared to take the credit for each other's achievements, and perhaps more strikingly, are more and more prepared to accept responsibility for each other's wrongs. Why should a British university student join a demonstration against the Vietnam war? Neither he nor his countrymen are suffering as a result of that war, and his country is not directly involved in it. It is because modern media of communication have made him aware of the plight of the Vietnamese peasant, and of the fact that he is being bombed out of his village, is having his children burnt to death with napalm and his fields made infertile with chemical sprays. And being aware, he cannot help feeling involved. And being involved, he cannot help feeling responsible, however little there may be that he can actually do.

We have an innate capacity to feel sympathy for other members of our community, and our communications media have brought the Vietnamese peasant, and the Biafran baby and the South African mineworker and many of the other underprivileged of earth, within the orbit of our awareness. They have brought them *into* our community and our instinctive sympathy takes over from there. They are all of them now 'my people'.

Granted, this feeling has its limitations. Not all of us feel like this. But an increasing number of us do. We feel responsible, and therefore we feel guilty, for what other human beings are suffering.

But are we not going a little too fast? I have suggested that at the popular level the notion of corporate responsibility carries a certain conviction. I have also shown that in certain contexts (as of government or law) it has practical usefulness. But is there not something basically irrational about it? Am I *right* to feel guilty about the plight of the Vietnamese peasant?

In answer I must first make again the statement that I have made several times before, that even if we were to prove that corporate guilt feelings are irrational it would not solve the problem. It is the guilt we do feel that creates the problem, not simply the guilt we ought to feel.

Common sense suggests that I am only responsbile for a situation if I can do something about it. Let us, for the moment, accept this, and see how it applies to the Vietnamese peasant or to the question of world poverty in general. In the face of these questions the individual feels helpless, but it is not true that he is *entirely* helpless. First, there is private charity. We can, if we care sufficiently, contribute to funds which will help the Vietnamese peasant, or others of the world's poor, which will, in the short term, buy food for them during famine, and in the long term help to provide needed capital equipment or practical instruction which will raise the productivity of their land. In proportion to the size of the problem the efforts of charitable organizations may be trivial, but they are not negligible.

Help on a really useful scale can only be provided by governments, and this is where the second possibility of real help comes in. The processes of decision-making in a modern democratic state are at least in principle open to influence. Minorities campaigning for unpopular causes are often sceptical about this, and they may well be right that governments are not responsive enough to public pressure, but if the pressure is strong enough, if a sufficiently large number of people are convinced of the importance of a cause, democratic governments are obliged, in the end, to take some notice. If our consciences are offended by what is going on in the impoverished two-thirds of the world, we have this possibility open to us, to educate the consciences of our fellow countrymen and to bring public opinion to bear on our government. This will doubtless be a long hard grind, but what is ultimately accomplished may be quite substantial.

Even if we begin, then, with the common-sense assumption that we are only responsible for a situation which we can help, we may be driven to the conclusion that we do share a genuine moral responsibility for such phenomena as world poverty. We cannot regard ourselves as free of that responsibility as long as there is a single thing left that we can do.

What most of us do is to attempt to discharge our feelings of guilt about such things by means of a token. We give a shilling a week to Oxfam, not because it really helps very much but because it makes us feel better. This is to treat the symptom, not the disease. We quieten the guilt feelings without having done anything substantial about the guilt, about the responsibility which we genuinely do share. In extreme instances the token may be something quite irrelevant to the need. After the Aberfan disaster, in which a colliery spoil heap collapsed on to a school, killing virtually all the children in it, there was an immense wave of public feeling. It was freely stated at the time that one component of this feeling was a feeling of guilt on the part of those who lived in more prosperous and salubrious areas of the country. Be that as it may, it was certainly a powerful feeling of sympathy. But it expressed itself in bizarre ways. People sent money; vast amounts of it in total. Most of this was not needed and has since proved a great embarrassment. But they also tried to convey their sympathy for the dead children by sending toys to the few survivors. Enormous numbers of teddy bears arrived in Aberfan. Why? They did not help anybody in Aberfan, but they did something for the consciences of those who sent them.

Public protest, too, is capable of being used in the same way, not as a means of achieving anything but to mollify the conscience. It is worth examining, at this point, the nature and function of public protest. By the phrase 'public protest' I do not only mean the more active sort of demonstration. One can make a public protest without going to Grosvenor Square and rolling marbles under the hooves of the police horses; by writing letters to the newspapers, for example. One may indulge in protest for dubious or downright bad reasons. One may join a demonstration for the sake of the excitement, as an excuse to let off steam; or because one has a taste for real violence; or for purely political reasons, because every step in the direction of anarchy is a blow at the capitalist system and brings the day of revolution nearer. One may write letters to the newspaper because one likes to see one's name in print.

But there are good reasons for protest too. Every protest is an assertion of concern. It is an attempt to bring the object of one's concern to the attention of one's fellows. It is an attempt to make people take notice, and hence an attempt to persuade. It is an attempt to change other people's moral priorities. It is part of the process of moral education.

There are instances in which a protest may be hopeless, and known to be hopeless. In these cases it is no more than a gesture, but it may be none the less important for that. The protester may be saying, in effect, 'I know you won't do anything about it. I don't really expect you to understand. But I am doing this to show you how I feel; how much it matters to *me*.' This idea is important and I shall come back to it in a later chapter.

One reason for a protest, and not only the hopeless kind, is to dissociate oneself from the actions or policies of one's society. Sometimes, when all attempts to convert one's fellows to one's own way of thinking have failed, this is all there is left to be done. It is as far as one can go in discharging oneself of communal responsibility. The classic instance of this is resignation from a committee or other body. When one has done one's best to persuade, and one's colleagues insist on a certain course of action, if one disapproves strongly enough, then the proper, the accepted way of expressing this, is by resignation. By resigning one is saying: 'This is not my decision. I have no part in it. I take no blame for it.' In certain situations this is an excellent solution. It genuinely exempts one from complicity and hence from guilt. But there are many situations in which the solution does not apply. If the policies of my government are felt to involve me, as an Englishman, in immorality and evil, I cannot resign from being English. But I may make such a protest as to demonstrate publicly that I disapprove, and dissociate myself, as far as it is possible to do so, from my government's action.

Perhaps we shall have to refine the common-sense principle with which we started. Even if the situation in which I am involved is one which I can do nothing effective to change, am I not morally obliged at least to make a protest? Even if I know that I am going to be outvoted and overruled, should not my conscience compel me to stand up and be counted? If I allow something that is morally objectionable to happen without protest, am I not guilty of complicity? I must surely be responsible to some degree for the sins of my society if I do not make my voice heard against them.

Societies may be blameworthy without there being many individuals among them who are positively corrupt. A society may tolerate slums, inequalities of all sorts, discrimination against minorities, without any of its members positively willing these things, but merely because not enough of them positively will to remove them. Such a society is no less truly corrupt than one which is based on oppression. It is corrupt by default, and all its members therefore guilty by default.

If only for this reason, capacity to do something about a situation cannot be the sole criterion of moral responsibility for it. Even when there is no possibility of influencing the situation, protest may be a moral duty.

But perhaps our common-sense principle needs further modification still, for are there not situations in which we all ack-

40

nowledge responsibility for acts which we could not influence since we were not there at the time? Let us take the simple case of the boy who breaks the next door neighbour's window. I do not know what the law says about this situation, but would not any civilized father feel morally bound to pay for the replacement of the window? He feels a certain responsibility for the action, though it was not committed by him and he could not have prevented it. We assume that parents are responsible for damage which their children do. The nature of the relationship between parents and child makes this assumption reasonable.

But take another example in which the relationship is much less close. I am travelling, let us say, in a foreign country. I encounter a man who is behaving rudely and inconsiderately to a third party. I feel disgusted. But then I discover that the rude and inconsiderate man is an Englishman. Immediately I experience quite a different emotion, in addition to my disgust. I feel ashamed. No one will think me odd if I go so far as to apologize for my countryman's behaviour, or try in some discreet way to make amends. I have never met this man before in my life: why should I feel responsible for the way he behaves? I feel responsible for no other reason than that he is my fellow countryman, and the vast majority of men would agree that I am right to do so.

There are circumstances, therefore, in which I not only feel sympathy for other human beings and a compulsion to assist them, a responsibility for them in that sense, but also a moral responsibility for their actions. I feel that what *they* have done has involved *me* in disgrace, brought the community to which we both belong into disrepute; that because of *their* action *I* ought to be ashamed. And as a corollary, that what *I* do may make amends for *their* fault.

Even in the twentieth century our sense of community is sufficiently strong to make such ideas seem to most of us to be self-evidently just. And our sense of community extends also to the past. It is commonly asserted that modern western man has no sense of history, no sense of continuity with the past. But this is not entirely true, as a single example may suffice to show.

It will scarcely be disputed that during the colonial era Britain (like other colonial nations) exploited her colonies. I am not going to argue all the pros and cons of this, and do not deny that the colonies in some respects derived benefit from the situation. The point of my argument is that we acknowledge that exploitation did go on, and that as a consequence of this Britain owes something to her colonies and ex-colonies. In practical terms, this means that the present generation of Englishmen is in debt to the present generation of Africans, etc., not for anything we have done to them, but for what our fathers did to their fathers. That we are morally responsible for this exploitation, or, in a word, guilty, is something which few Englishmen, and even fewer Africans, would deny.

Thus the notion of corporate guilt, corporate responsibility, of guilt transferred from generation to generation or from individual to community, is not merely an archaic belief found in ancient myths and legends and among primitive peoples. It is an idea which in many contexts we treat as reasonable.

Residual guilt

We have reached two main conclusions. As an individual, there are actions of mine, many of them habitual actions, which I would like to be able to control but cannot entirely do so. There are aspects of my personality which I might wish were different, but I cannot successfully do much about them. These are things which I cannot properly control. But I cannot help the feeling that I *ought* to be able to control them. I feel guilty about them, and even on reflection, having made all the allowances, I cannot get rid of the belief that I am, at least in a measure, morally responsible, genuinely guilty.

I also feel guilty about many things that are wrong in my society. Some of these I can do a little to set right. Where I can do nothing practical I can at least protest; I can dissociate myself as far as possible from the actions and policies of which I disapprove. But when I have done everything, I still feel that I am involved in moral responsibility, in guilt. And again, even

42

on reflection I cannot convince myself that I am unreasonable in doing so.

There is a passage in the book of Leviticus (Lev. 6) in which regulations are laid down concerning the expiation of certain types of crimes. When a man 'has deceived his neighbour in a matter of deposit or security, or through robbery, or if he has oppressed his neighbour, or has found what was lost and lied about it, swearing falsely', he must first make full amends to the man whom he has wronged, and add a surcharge of twenty per cent. And then he must offer a guilt-offering, a sacrifice to God. When the offender has done everything that can reasonably be done to compensate for his crime, something remains, or is felt to remain, which can only be expiated by cultic means. Is this not a widespread human conviction, that when one has taken all reasonable steps to make amends, something remains to be lived down, there is still something to be forgiven? When the damage done by the misdeed has been repaired, as far as it is humanly possible to repair it, there is still a residual guilt which we *feel*.

Maybe this is an irrational feeling. Maybe its biological origin can be accounted for, but the feelings themselves cannot be removed by rational argument. They can only be removed by something which the sufferer is able to regard as an act of expiation, by a symbolic cleansing, by a sprinkling of blood, or by the receiving of a sacrament, or by some other act which expresses the conviction that something has been offered, or something done, to blot out that residual stain.

There will be readers who respond to what I have just been saying with the thought: *I* don't have these residual feelings of guilt. I'm not obsessed by guilt feelings, rational or irrational. And if I do anything I regret, I apologize or make amends as well as I can, and that's that. As to any corporate responsibility: I feel disgusted at what goes on in Vietnam, or eastern Nigeria and all the other horror spots. I do what I can in the way of charity, and I'd vote for any candidate who promised to fight in parliament for humane policies on the part of our government. But having said this, I've done all that is possible. My only

43

residual feeling is one of agonized sympathy for the sufferers whom I cannot help further.

I have three things to say in reply. First, if you feel like this, there are a lot of other people like you. Guilt feelings are not, in ordinary circumstances, your problem. And it is a pity that the western Christian tradition, in framing its presentation of the gospel almost exclusively in terms of guilt and forgiveness, has largely overlooked the needs of the people of your sort.

Second, at least concede that there are people who *are* guilt-ridden; for whom the chronic insecurity of most of humankind takes the form of feelings of guilt. And for people of this kind, guilt is a very large problem indeed.

Third, those of us who do not feel overcome with guilt may even be in the majority, but we do, most of us, feel threatened in other ways, and our insecurity tends to express itself in other forms. Some of these we shall now examine.

NOTES

1. Arthur Miller, *Collected Plays*, New York: Viking Press, 1957.
2. On this whole question see G. K. Galbraith, *The Affluent Society*, London: Hamish Hamilton, 1958, especially chs. 9 and 24.

3 Man under Pressure

Though the western Christian tradition has spoken chiefly in terms of sin and guilt, and has seen salvation principally as the forgiveness of sins, this is not true of other branches of the Christian tradition, and is not entirely true of the New Testament. The New Testament does talk of salvation in terms of forgiveness and reconciliation, but it talks just as much in terms of redemption from bondage, and above all, of healing. It is perhaps fair to say that in the gospels the typical image of the saved man is the whole man, the healthy man. In the epistles the saved man is the man who has found freedom.

The terms in which the New Testament speaks of bondage may at first sight seem remote from twentieth-century life. The New Testament writers think of man as being under the domination of numerous 'powers', occult forces which control the cosmos and corrupt it. Christ came to conquer the powers and to free men from them.

This does not look like a very useful approach. No one today could seriously believe in the existence of the 'powers'. But does not modern man share New Testament man's experience in that he sometimes feels himself to be the prey of forces beyond his control? Twentieth-century man and first-century man analyse this experience in different ways and arrive at different rationalizations of it, but the underlying experience that is being interpreted is a universal one. Twentieth-century man sees these forces as forces within his own *psyche*, elements of his own personality. Or he sees them as forces within society. They are mysterious forces only in that they are ill-understood and difficult to control. First-century man (and ancient man in general) was very ready to give these forces a separate and distinct existence of their own. He personalized them; turned them into superhuman beings or influences, and identified them with demons, devils and astral powers.

Now as we shall see towards the end of this chapter, modern man is not a total stranger to this tendency to personalize or give independent existence to the forces that oppress him. But when he does so, he knows very well that this is just a way of talking. Ancient man, on the other hand, appears to have taken such language literally.

What we are going to do next is to explore this common experience of being threatened, or overwhelmed, to see if we can pick out some of the roots from which it springs.

Inadequacy

A sense of inadequacy is well-nigh universal. Nobody, of course, except the outright neurotics (though quite a lot of us *are* outright neurotics) feels inadequate all the time. But most of us are from time to time assailed by such feelings. Things 'get on top of us'.

This can happen at a very simple level. Some of us lead fairly complicated lives – more complicated, at any rate, than we can easily cope with. And occasionally the complications are just too much; we have too many things to remember, too many things to do and too many other people to please. There are mornings when we wake up and before we even get our eyes open all the things that have to be done come crowding into our minds, and we know that today we just aren't going to make it.

This mundane problem, of getting through the day or the week without getting into a frightful mess, may seem relatively trivial. But to the man (or woman) facing it the problem is mountainous. It saps emotional energy, destroys self-confidence. The accumulation of relatively minor derelictions, letters we never got round to answering, people we ought to have seen and never did, phone calls that we needn't have put off – goodness knows, they would only have taken a few seconds, but we left them until it was too late – over a long time can erode the very substance of the personality, until we look inside ourselves and there is nothing left, except a massive sense of failure.

Though it may show itself in trivial things, this inability to cope with life is very serious, and in a world that is becoming increasingly more complex it becomes increasingly common. And as the world becomes increasingly competitive, individuals are tempted to push themselves too close to the limits of their abilities. Our ambitions (or other people's ambitions for us) drive us on, until we have the satisfaction of achieving jobs which are really too difficult for us to do, or which we can do only by continuing to drive ourselves.

And even if a man's job is not actually too difficult for him to manage, it may still leave him too little margin for safety. He may cope with a somewhat difficult job successfully as long as his family life is stable. He may manage a turbulent family life as long as he is not over-taxed at work. But as soon as there is trouble in both situations, war on two fronts, he collapses. And the demands of modern life are such that more and more of us are finding ourselves in such situations.

Let us look in more detail at one or two of the particular areas in which our inadequacy is most keenly felt.

Sex

The sex instinct is one of the most powerful and primitive of human urges. It is also the one which can most quickly lead us into trouble with our fellows if freely indulged. In a civilized society, therefore, it has to be suppressed or controlled for most of the time. It is therefore a powerfully emotive subject, surrounded by more social taboos than any other, and responsible for more phobias, guilt-feelings and anxieties than any other phenomenon in human experience.

We are always telling each other how unhealthily reticent the Victorians were about sex. We, with our more open attitudes, have come to terms with the matter far more effectively. What rubbish! We are as neurotic about sex as any society there has ever been. We suffer just as much anxiety on the subject as the Victorians ever did. We have changed the nature of the anxiety, that is all. The Victorian's anxiety showed itself in the guise of morality. He felt guilty if he contemplated the subject at all. Our anxieties show themselves for the most part as worries about sexual inadequacy.

Novelists, film-makers, playwrights and the press have got us convinced that the 'normal' human being is a sexual libertine, and probably a pervert. Among the characters in television plays promiscuity seems to be the norm rather than the exception. The ideal of all males is taken to be the man who 'makes' all the girls. Ann Jellicoe's play *The Knack*[1] is a first-rate exposition, to the point of parody, of this notion. Its central character, Tolan, is the man who in their fantasy lives all men are supposed to want to be. Tolan is a bachelor. But he has a bed six feet wide. (In the background is a legendary character called Rory McBride, who never actually appears, and who may be the projection of Tolan's own fantasy. Rory McBride has an eight-foot bed.)

Now the normal man is not by any means as sex-ridden as the professional communicators would like us to believe. But the professional communicators have got the normal man worried. They have got him more than half convinced that all the other normal men *are* sex-ridden, so the normal man is anxious, suspects that he isn't normal after all, feels sexually inadequate. The single man is made to feel a failure because he doesn't get enough girls. The men in the telly plays are always meeting very fetching girls who quickly turn out to be near-nympho-maniacs: but *he* never does. And the married man is no better off, because he has been led to believe that sex should dominate marriage, and when he finds that it doesn't he imagines he's missing something.

The psychologists, who are sometimes as dreadful a breed of insecurity mongers as the advertisers, have told him that the sexual act, properly undertaken, involves an emotional fulfil-ment too profound for words, and an emotional satisfaction which is immeasurably rich and strange. Now we all know that they are right (give or take a purple passage or two). But nobody has told the normal man that there is a place in marriage for sexual restraint, and that such restraint can sometimes be as much an expression of love as indulgence. And this stress on the sexual ideal has meant that ninety-nine per cent of the people who listen to psychologists are dissatisfied, quite unnecessarily, with their sex lives.

The anxiety mongers are waiting to cash in on our discontent. Miss X has reached the advanced age of twenty, and she hasn't a boy friend. Is there something wrong with her, that even her best friends won't tell her? The anxiety mongers will sell her deodorants and toothpaste, or an uplift bra, on the strength of her worry. What they are really selling, of course, is confidence, balm for Miss X's self-esteem, healing for her bruised soul. They are selling salvation. And in the process they play on her sense of inadequacy.

The family

There are no successful parents. Every parent knows what is meant by a sense of inadequacy. Every day, in a multitude of ways, he feels that he is letting his children down. Everybody tells him so. The children themselves are the most effective anxiety-mongers here. They leave him in no doubt that other children's parents are superior in every way. They give their children more pocket money, let them stay up later, let them watch more television, take them out oftener, live in nicer houses, have more time to spare for their offspring, go to better places for their holidays, and are altogether nicer people to know.

The psychologists don't improve matters by disagreeing among themselves, but when they do agree it is only to demand of the poor parent that he accomplish the impossible. He emerges from the reading of child psychology convinced that he is much too strict with his children, and much too lax; that he is also far too inconsistent; that he ought to spend at least twenty-five hours a day playing with his children, reading to them, supervising their activities, talking to them and generally stimulating them, and must also allow them more time to themselves, to develop, to express their own personalities. He must not hamper them in any way, force his own ideas on them, try to

49

make them fit into his own mould, but he must give them firm guidance and a sound set of standards and principles to live by.

Every parent is aware that he does not provide his children with proper educational opportunities, that he is failing to allow the child to make the best of his abilities. If he had not already got the message from all those articles on education that keep appearing in the national press, and from the things the headmaster keeps on saying at the parent-teacher association meetings, and from those excellent education programmes which one sees on television, then the man who came round last week selling encyclopaedias at the door would have enlightened him.

The message of all this is crystal clear. Everybody is agreed. And they leave the parent himself in no doubt. He is a failure.

The problem of loving

The one thing that no parent can do nowadays is to talk to his own children. He cannot express what he really feels. He cannot say to them what he really thinks. And this is only one aspect of his inadequacy in human relations. Some of us are chronically unable to express what we really feel, even to those closest to us; indeed, especially to those closest to us.

Some of us can't talk to our wives: can't talk, that is, about anything that really matters. We can't tell them that we love them; not in so many words, because we'd be embarrassed. And when we try to do it in other ways it doesn't seem to get through.

These are very common problems. We are not good at expressing our emotions, or if we manage it at all, we do it in such different ways that we misunderstand each other. A wife, perhaps, wants to be brought flowers occasionally, and have her wedding anniversary remembered, and to the husband it never occurs that such things are really important. He may try to express his affection by bringing cups of tea in bed or helping around the house, and is hurt when these gestures don't appear to count. We have to learn not only to offer affection, but to give it in the way it is required. It is no good offering it in the wrong package, because it isn't recognized. It is no good expressing it beautifully, but in a code whose nuances are not appreciated by the recipient.

These are just a few examples of the common ways in which we fail in our human relationships. There are certainly few of us who are very successful in this field. Even those who manage to be highly successful in other areas frequently fail in this one.

Ambition

We all begin with big ideas of what we might do and what we might become. Our adult life consists in a process of coming to terms with reality. The big ideas of youth are cut down to size. We come to accept our limitations.

This is not a continuous process. There are usually a number of critical points or experiences, with longer periods of equanimity in between. Middle life, at least for a man, is often associated with a kind of second adolescence. He has to go again through the process of discovering his own identity. He takes stock of himself in a more realistic way than before. The man who is emotionally immature may, when faced with this experience, develop a bitterness about his limited achievements (for whose limitations he may blame everybody but himself), or he may become disillusioned about himself and his prospects, living the rest of his life oppressed by his own failure. Or he may refuse to face up to reality at all, and persist in dreams of the big success he will still make, or credit himself with successes that are largely imaginary. (On this last theme see Arthur Miller's pathetic exploration in *Death of a Salesman*.)[2]

The man going through this process of readjustment may try to recapture his lost youth, reverting to pastimes which gave him satisfaction when he was in his teens. George Orwell comments perceptively, and very amusingly, on this device in his novel *Coming up for Air*.[3] An even commoner resort is for the man to boost his self-confidence by attracting a mistress. This characteristically happens in a man's middle forties and is very frequently a sign of the 'second adolescence'.

51

The man of more mature mind may toy with one or more of these moods or devices but passes through them. The end result is to readjust his image of himself. And such adjustment may not be entirely passive. He may decide that some mistakes he has made it may not be too late to set right. This can be upsetting for his own family, to whom it may look like a sudden change of character. The whole process necessarily involves great upheaval. The acute feelings of failure which it brings may pass, or they may be more or less permanent.

The problem of coming to terms with oneself is made much worse by the fact that we live in an increasingly competitive world. 'The rat race' is an unpleasant phrase; all the more unpleasant because of the accuracy with which it represents the facts of twentieth-century life. Few of us have the strength to opt out (and we reserve our nastiest feelings for those who successfully do so.) In such a world, where only the man at the top is a total success, everbody else is a comparative failure. A competitive system feeds on failure and fosters failure. A world in which the winner takes all is a world in which bitterness and disillusion must abound.

Even the successful are, for the most part, only *comparatively* successful. The £2,000 a year man feels a failure because he isn't earning £3,000. The £3,000 a year man feels a failure because he has his eye on £4,000 a year jobs which are out of his reach – and so on.

Perhaps, some day, we shall evolve a humane system which gives everyone the self-respect which comes from succeeding, or at least, which doesn't over-value the people who do things *best*. We are so obsessed by the superlative performance that we no longer get pleasure out of the comparatively good. We can't enjoy the local operatic society's production because we heard the world's best singers do the same thing on the telly last week. We make the youngster who is learning the piano feel that if he doesn't make concert pianist grade it isn't worth going on with it, and the young swimmer that if he is never likely to break a world record he might as well give it up. Perhaps some day we shall learn the truth of Chesterton's dictum that if a thing is worth doing it is worth doing badly. But at the moment we affect to despise the man who has not the will to push his capacities to their very limits, and to admire the one who sacrifices everything for one chosen ambition. We are all failures, for we set such a premium on success.

Redundancy

I do not use this word simply to refer to problems like what to do with thousands of highly skilled miners on a coalfield where all the pits are closed. Such problems, and they are acute enough, and bitter enough for the people involved, are nevertheless only one aspect of a much wider problem.

It used to be, in all ages until this one, that as a man's natural vigour abated and his capacity for work, in this sense, declined he made up in skill and experience what he lost in strength and speed. Experience was the one valuable asset he acquired with age, even though he lost others. But in a society which is changing as rapidly as ours experience becomes devalued. Experience implies to some extent fixed habits of mind, and these are an increasing disadvantage. My experience, which I so prize, is experience of a world which has already passed away, and of conditions which will not come again. The skill which I have so laboriously acquired may be made valueless tomorrow by the invention of a new machine, a change in fashion, or the discovery of a cheap substitute for the thing I am engaged in manufacturing.

The young are ready enough at the best of times to imagine that wisdom belongs to them. In the present age they seem to have abundant justification for their belief. It is widely assumed by them that age, experience, tradition and history can be written off. They are simply not relevant in a world where new situations, new problems, and new solutions to the old ones, new techniques and new institutions, appear as regularly as the morning milk.

The older generation is thus faced with a fear which it never faced in history before. It is terrified of its own young. It is denied one of the historic compensations of maturity and age, respect. Highly skilled men find themselves employed in unskilled work. They are too old to retrain, too old to learn. Men feel constantly out of their depth in a world which they should be in a position to control.

The fear of redundancy strikes at the basis of human personality. 'Redundant' means 'unwanted'. And 'unwanted' means, at least for the heart, 'unloved'.

Corporate inadequacy

There is another way in which many of us today feel our inadequacy. We feel inadequate not simply as individuals, but as a society. We are disillusioned about the capacity of human beings to solve the world's problems. We are aware that wealth abounds, as it has never done in the world's history, and yet that millions live (and die) in such poverty that they cannot buy enough to eat. We have a passionate desire for peace. And yet we spend a ridiculous proportion of our resources in developing weapons of mass destruction. We all agree on the need for toleration and goodwill. Yet public manifestations of hatred and prejudice are everywhere.

Once we believed it was only a matter of time; that progress was inevitable, and that common sense, at least, if not universal love, was bound in the end to prevail. But now no longer. We no longer believe in the capacity of the human race to manage its own affairs. We cannot trust it not to destroy itself. It seems unable to accomplish even those necessary ends that are vital to its survival.

We have rediscovered the power of evil and the impotence of reason. On a corporate, a racial level, we have come back to St Paul's experience of moral impotence. The good that we want to do, we cannot; and the evil that we do not want is what we do. Doubtless this feeling is not universal, but it is prevalent enough.

The nightmare

For all the reasons I have mentioned, and no doubt for some others, a feeling of inadequacy is common. We all occasionally

54

have the feeling of living in a world that is too big for us, too complicated for us to cope with; of running in a race in which the pace is too hot. This can play on the imagination, so that we project our felt inadequacies on to the world around us. We feel threatened.

Man has always felt this. The theme of threat appears in his dreams, his fairy tales, his myths, his music. It is a common theme of art. And it is something to which we can all respond, because it is familiar. We have all had nightmares. And some of us have experienced the worst nightmare of all, the sort from which we wake up, only to discover that it is real.

Modern technology and expertise does not remove the sense of threat, because as fast as one problem is overcome, another appears. Science and technology themselves provide new ones. The theme of a great deal of science fiction is that of the disaster triggered off by man's own technology, of unknown and uncontrollable forces released by human meddling with the universe.

And even though it is true that many of the external threats to our existence have been removed or reduced, the unknown and uncontrollable forces *within* still frighten us, the ones within our own personalities, or within our society. It is true that we know and control progressively more and more, but still from beyond the boundaries of the safe, assured world, come the marauders.

The humorist, Paul Jennings, wrote an essay[4] in which he invented a new philosophy, called Resistentialism – or, since these things always sound more impressive in a foreign language, *Resistenzialismus* or *résistentialisme*. Its motto, or principle, was *Les choses sont contre nous*. The universe is against us. The world of things, said Jennings, is in league against mankind. He even devised an experimental proof of the resistentialist principle: that if a large number of slices of bread and butter are dropped, one by one, and at random, on a carpet (and for the purposes of this experiment the more expensive the carpet the better), a statistically significant proportion of them, i.e. significantly more than fifty per cent, will land *butter side down*.

Which of us does not feel the appeal of Resistentialism? We

are all thoroughly acquainted with the cussedness of things. If the car breaks down, it is always miles from anywhere. If the kids get measles, it is always the day before we go on holiday. If the milkman doesn't call, it is inevitably the morning we are giving a coffee party. But which of us would have thought of elevating it into philosophy?

The same theme of threat appears in our literature. Probably the best known exponent of it is Franz Kafka. His unfinished novel *The Trial*[5] is an outstanding example of his methods. Joseph K. is threatened with prosecution. He does not know of what crime he is accused. He is given only the vaguest indication of the system by which he will be tried or the means whereby he may defend himself. Since he does not know of what he is accused, even he himself cannot say whether he is innocent or guilty.

A similar theme appears occasionally in the work of Vladimir Nabokov. Nabokov's early novel, *Invitation to a Beheading*,[6] is an interesting parallel to Kafka's *The Trial*. It has a similar nightmare quality, but a more hopeful ending. Nabokov's hero, Cincinnatus, knows what he is accused of, and has no doubts about his guilt. Cincinnatus is opaque, in a country where all men are transparent. The forces of justice play cat and mouse with Cincinnatus, and not only enjoy thsemselves thoroughly in the process but fail to understand why the mouse does not. And at the end Cincinnatus has the bad taste to spoil the game.

Though Nabokov's novel is in the end a powerful statement of faith, whereas Kafka's is a statement of despair, the two agree remarkably well in their presentation of the human predicament. The real phenomenon that provides the material for both the Kafka and the Nabokov nightmares is the totalitarian state. But even the benevolent state can present the same picture to bewildered man. One ingredient in the nightmare of the modern world is bureaucracy: the man we want to see is always on his holidays, or interviewing another client, and will we please wait. And when at last we manage to see the man, there is always a regulation that says that this is the affair of a different department, or that we haven't fulfilled the necessary conditions – and in the end that nothing can be done.

A more recent literary exposition of this theme is Joseph Heller's *Catch 22*.[7] There is always a catch somewhere, and for Heller it is always catch 22. Catch 22 is the small print on the other side of the page; though the customer never has a chance to read it, because only 'They' are allowed to know what it says. If you want to know what it says you have to ask 'Them'. And it says whatever 'They' want it to say, and 'They' are the sole arbiters of what it means.

Examples could be multiplied. George Orwell's *Nineteen Eighty-four*[8] and David Karp's *One*[9] spring readily to mind. All the examples are fantasy, but fantasy that rings true because it corresponds horribly closely to what things sometimes feel like in reality. We have a popular catchword which sums up the feeling exactly. 'You can't win.' We say it ruefully, half playfully, but it expresses a feeling which is serious enough, that some superior power has loaded the dice against us. And the feeling is not so far removed from that of New Testament man, when he spoke of the tyranny of the Powers, the Thrones, Dominions, Principalities and Authorities, the world rulers of this present darkness. We do not believe in the literal existence of such forces, but we are familiar enough with the feelings which they represent, and we share the apostle's conviction that 'we are not contending against flesh and blood', but against the Machine, against the System, against the nameless, faceless 'Them' in high places.

Something to hate

Expressing our anxieties in art, drama, literature, etc., may help us to deal with them and to come to terms with them, but there is another, less pleasant method of expressing them that may perhaps make them worse. We can look for someone to blame. We can project our anxieties and frustrations on to someone else, blaming them for our failures, our inadequacies, the things that go wrong.

This type of response is the father of the conspiracy theory of

57

history. In its extreme form it sees everything as a plot. Every untoward happening, every disliked feature of contemporary life, every hiatus in the ordered fabric of existence, is ascribed to the Red menace, or the Jewish menace, or the Catholic menace, or the Blacks.

All this, though its effects are (if I may put it in such a restrained fashion) often undesirable, has its roots in a real need of the human spirit. Some anonymous sage once enunciated the requirements for human happiness as, 'Something to do, something to love, and something to hope for'. If he had been a cynical sage he might have added, 'And something to hate'. George Orwell, who was a very perceptive observer of the political animal, foresaw in his *Nineteen Eighty-four* the totalitarian state resorting to the device of keeping the populace contented by working up synthetic hatred against Goldstein and the Brotherhood. The idea was not Orwell's own invention. Communist societies have stirred up hatred against 'counter-revolutionaries' or 'revisionists' in exactly this way, using the notion of conspiracy to foster solidarity among the faithful. The Marxists themselves learnt the technique from the church, which inculcated among its members a horror of heresy and heretics in the same fashion. And the church had the Old Testament to inspire it; the Old Testament which, amongst all its fine humanitarian laws and principles, insists on total hatred of all who tempt Israel to the worship of foreign gods or idols.[10]

Why are human beings such a ready prey to this device? It is partly, as I have already suggested, that we find it congenial to blame someone or something else for our failures and inadequacies, and to project our guilt feelings on to others. But it is partly because human beings need a sense of identity. They need to know where they belong. And one way of establishing one's own identity and defining one's own circle is by drawing a hard and fast line between those who belong and those who do not; by pointing to clearly marked differences between 'us' and 'them'; and, usually, by emphasizing the superiority of 'us'. It seems almost that men need to despise in order to be.

58

In our cosmopolitan modern world the problem of identity is becoming is some ways more acute. It is becoming increasingly obvious that for most practical purposes the human race is a single society. Finding someone to hate outside our society is therefore increasingly difficult, so we find our *bête noir* within it.

From our present point of view this phenomenon is interesting as another example of the way in which human beings express their feelings of being threatened. They identify the forces of evil with some group of their fellows which may be relatively easy to define, like 'The Jews', or 'The Pakistanis', or so nebulous as almost to defy identification, like 'The Capitalists', 'The Bourgeoisie', or 'The Lefties'.

Pseudo-salvation

Just as the feelings of being threatened, oppressed, or inadequate are common, so is the belief that somewhere there is a kind of magic talisman that could put it all right. This is the belief that men of the early Christian centuries (pagan men as well as Christians) would have recognized as the belief in salvation. Salvation is the one thing that would get us out of the mess, the one thing that would make life wonderful, the one thing after which we should need no other things, after which we should be content.

Salvation takes different forms in the imagination of different people. For a good many in Britain salvation is a big win on the Treble Chance. But for most of us salvation is something which is easier of attainment, but which we know in our realistic moments will be devalued as soon as we have it. For the man with raging toothache the one thing that will make life beautiful again is having the tooth out. For the time being, that is salvation. For the woman with four small children under five years old, salvation is getting them all off to school. 'It will be all right then.' It will be salvation. Salvation is whatever you imagine is going to 'make it all right'. For some of us, however much or however little we have, salvation will always be a twenty percent rise.

Original sin?

I have established, I hope, the ubiquity of a sense of guilt and/or failure and inadequacy. Few of us feel these things all the time, but very nearly all of us feel them some of the time. Not only as individuals do we feel guilty or inadequate. We feel that we are bound up in a society of guilty and inadequate men. Our society as a whole is no more able than our individual selves to cope with the problems of life. And just as we, as individuals, have sometimes done things which we ourselves disapprove of, because we could not help ourselves, so society does things and allows things which none of its members positively desires.

So, we not only have feelings of guilt and inadequacy, but we are convinced that these are not illusory, or not entirely. They are not simply the product of uncontrollable depression. In some respects, both as individuals and as a society, we *are* guilty, we *are* inadequate. This is not a problem that can be shrugged off. It is an impasse. And it is important. To say that man is guilty, and a failure, is to say one of the most important things that can be said about him. It is to point to an ineradicable feature of the human condition. Man, just because he is a man, shares these qualities. They are inextricably bound up with his humanity.

It is interesting to find an atheistic writer like Albert Camus presenting the same sort of conclusions. Camus' novel *The Fall*,[11] if I have rightly understood it, is a statement of the very fact I have set out above, that if we wish to understand what man is we must see him first of all as guilty.

William Golding, in his own characteristic way, has repeatedly probed the question of guilt and its origins. Golding, on his own admission, is a religious man, but the significant thing is that he has found it possible to explore the question of guilt in non-religious, or at least non-theistic terms, and that non-believers have responded to this. Atheistic and agnostic critics have acknowledged that Golding's picture of the human condition makes sense.

So then, without bringing God into the picture at all, we may reasonably argue that human guilt and inadequacy are facts, that they are important facts, and that they need to be faced. When modern man has these insights into his condition he is simply feeling what all men have occasionally felt. What is different about modern man is that he no longer puts a religious interpretation on his feelings, or resorts to religious methods of dealing with them.

Anyone acquainted with Christianity, however, will hardly need to have it pointed out to him how closely this picture of man as a guilty being agrees with traditional orthodoxy. Christian orthodoxy states that man is first and foremost a sinner. He is inevitably a sinner. He was born with the tendency to sin, in him. He is part of a society of men, a race, which is sinful, and he cannot escape responsibility for the sinfulness of the race as a whole. Mankind as a whole, and all individual men, need salvation.

It is a great pity that orthodoxy has often been expressed in terms which are nowadays easily misunderstood. Christians have traditionally represented these truths pictorially by talking about the sin of Adam, the founder of the human race, who involved all his descendants in responsibility for his transgression and who transmitted to them the sinful propensity which they all inherit. Stated in this form the idea is unacceptable. We cannot concede that, even if Adam had historically existed, which he did not, it would make sense to say that his descendants must bear responsibility for his fault. Neither can we concede that Adam's sinful act could cause a tendency to sin to be transmitted, biologically, to his descendants. It is true that Christians of former times did believe that this was how our present situation arose. And some of them identified the physical sexual act as the means whereby original sin was passed on from generation to generation. But their belief in a historical Adam and a historical fall, in the handing on of responsibility from that historical individual to the rest of us, and in the biological transmission of his sinful propensity to the rest of the human race, are, as it were, accidental features of the system. These are the ways in which men of former times visualized the mechanics of the process. We can abandon these features of their theories without loss, as long as we recognize what it is they are trying to say. The traditional doctrine of original sin enshrines profound insights into the nature of man, insights to which modern man is not a stranger. We have abandoned religion, and are having painfully to rediscover truths which Christianity has been teaching all along.

There *is*, of course, a difference between traditional orthodoxy and modern secular interpretations of the problem of guilt, and a difference that is material. Christian orthodoxy does bring God into the picture. Man is guilty, says Christian orthodoxy, because he has sinned against his God. He needs salvation, because he has fallen short of what God intended him to be.

But the important point is this: the Christian places a theistic interpretation on the problem of guilt and failure because he happens to believe in God, it is not his belief in God which raises or creates the problem. The problems of human guilt and inadequacy are rooted in the nature of man; the theist will interpret them theistically and the atheist atheistically, but to opt for an atheistic interpretation does not dispose of the problem. The characteristic form in which Christianity has stated the problem of guilt and the human need for salvation has been determined by Christianity's characteristic beliefs, in God, in Christ, and in the Holy Spirit. The rejection of Christian beliefs, and therefore of the Christian statement of the problem, has led many to assume that the problem has been done away with; that if the idea of sin against a personal God be dispensed with, then the notion of guilt, or at least of original guilt, loses all meaning. But it is my contention that even if we have difficulties with the traditional Christian statement of the problem, the problem itself remains. We are entitled to conclude, if we think the evidence merits this conclusion, that the Christian doctrine of salvation through Christ is not an adequate answer to the problem, but we may not decide that the problem itself is an Aunt Sally which Christianity has erected.

It is true that Christians have sometimes deliberately set out to inculcate a sense of guilt into those whom they wished to convert. And it may be true that they have not always done this very intelligently or very fairly. But Christians have done this, not in an attempt to create a problem where none existed, but in the belief that they were making their converts aware of what the problems really were. I do not think they have always been wrong in this.

The other side of the coin

So far I have talked a lot about guilt and inadequacy. I make no apology. That is what this book is supposed to be about. But I do not want to give the impression that I believe there is no more to human nature than this. Christians have too often made it appear that they take a wholly pessimistic view of man. To say that man is guilty, and that this is a most important fact about him is true. But it is by no means the whole truth.

We may sometimes have uncontrolled bad impulses. But we have very many good ones too. Hatred comes all too naturally to us. But nothing is more natural than love. We have inborn tendencies to selfishness: but also inborn capacities for sympathy and trust. Our society may not be perfect, but for nearly all of the time we live together peaceably, inoffensively, each curbing his own appetites, ambitions and lawless impulses for the sake of harmony. If there are certain ineradicable deficiencies in human nature there are also certain ineradicable virtues. Almost all of us are capable, given the right circumstances, of self-sacrifice. Even the worst of men can show courage. And even among the worst of men courage is still a virtue. And we can all laugh at ourselves. Perhaps the last and most tenacious virtue of all is the capacity not to take ourselves too seriously. Albert Camus, whose book *The Fall* I quoted in defence of my exposition of guilt, ends another of his novels[12] with the restrained verdict that 'there are more things to admire in man than to despise'. Amen.

No view of man is accurate or useful if it fails to recognize not only his inadequacies and deficiencies but his astonishing accomplishments. He does at times feel guilty and a failure, sometimes justifiably. But at least as frequently he congratulates himself on his successes. Man is constantly suprising himself with his own achievements. Or perhaps it would be better to say, men are constantly being suprised at *each other's* achievements and expertise. I find myself astonished at the (presumably fairly simple) skills of the AA patrolman, who cures in seconds a problem that had me baffled for an hour. We are all astonished at the more frightening skills of the surgeon, or the more recondite ones of the biochemist.

These achievements of others, achievements of the human race as a whole, for some of us only highlight our private failures. Or they provide a sad comment on the corporate failure of nations to solve rather ordinary problems, like making sure that everybody has enough to eat. But not everyone reacts to them in this way. Mankind's successes are seen by many as a reason for optimism. It is only a matter of time, they think, of applying existing techniques more efficiently and inventing a few new ones, and *all* problems will be solved.

There are some of us, however, who, though we are as convinced as the optimists are that all problems are in principle capable of solution, suspect such flaws in human nature that the necessary resources will never be brought to bear. The quarrel between those who are optimistic about the future of man and those who are pessimistic is basically a conflict between those who are impressed by man's capacity to find the means and those who are frightened by his incapacity to determine the ends. Our present civilization is very strong on means. We can do anything, if we set our minds to it. But we are not very good at deciding what we should set our minds to. The people who really frighten me are the people who enthuse about the technical means and insist on regarding the ends as obvious. Now more than ever do we need theologians and philosophers and prophets (secular as well as religious) and as many other men of goodwill as possible, to insist on raising again and again the question of ends. Economists, sociologists, politicians and scientists of all sorts all have their own special brands of expertise, and all of them seem reluctant to face the question of what ends their techniques are to serve. Or if they are not reluctant to face it, they dismiss the question as having so obvious an answer that it is foolish to raise it at all. When they do discuss ends rather than means, when they discuss values, they sometimes show themselves to be hair-raisingly simple-minded about the matter.

Now theologians and philosophers have no special expertise at all, except in the asking of awkward questions, and a certain acquaintance with the answers that men in past generations have offered themselves. But this is precisely why they are needed now, to ask us what our objects are, what we are aiming at, what sort of society we really want to create, what sort of people we really want to be.

The historians ought to be able to help, for they can bear witness that societies have not always accepted the values that we regard as so unquestionable, that they have frequently pursued ends quite different from those pursued by ourselves, and that there is nothing to indicate that our aims are self-authenticating in a way that theirs were not.

To their discredit it must be admitted that it is not the theologians who are raising these questions in the most challenging way. The people who are most effectively challenging the values of our society are the hippies and such similar groups. And we hate them for this very reason, that if they are right, then we are living for the wrong things, and wasting a vast amount of time and nervous energy, not to mention the only lifetime we have got to spend, in the pursuit of an illusory and unsatisfactory existence. The theologian may write books questioning the values of his society, but then he goes back to his suburban home with its ninety-per-cent mortgage and worries about his chances of promotion, just like all the other men.

The point I am trying to make is excellently illustrated by the moon landings. Nothing could demonstrate better the capacity of human beings to accomplish what they set their hearts on, and their equal capacity to set their hearts on the wrong things. The moon landings are, of course, magnificent. But to the under-privileged, undernourished two-thirds of the world they are a magnificent irrelevance. We are clever enough to reach the moon, but not sensible enough to share out the world's resources with anything approaching equity.

c

Or to take another example: if there is a shipwreck, or a mine disaster, hundreds of thousands of pounds will cheerfully be spent on search and rescue operations while there is even a small chance of anyone being left alive to save. Yet whenever the road traffic regulations are made a shade more stringent, or anyone suggests further restrictions on drinking and driving, improvements which might save a hundred lives at the cost of a little inconvenience or a little expense to us all, there is a public outcry. Human beings are generous and enlightened, and also stupidly immoral, *at the same time*.

A proper view of man must take account of both aspects of his nature. His glory and his depravity have to be held in tension. However onesided in their presentation of man some elements in the Christian tradition may have been, the bible itself keeps a very careful balance. According to the biblical picture man is lord of creation, God's partner and regent, made only 'a little lower than God, and crowned with glory and honour'.[13] And yet at the same time, 'every imagination of his heart is only evil continually';[14] he is 'born in iniquity' and in sin did his mother conceive him;[15] and his heart 'is deceitful above all things and desperately wicked'.[16]

Man tends to be knocked off balance both by his achievements and by his failures. He is sometimes led on from a legitimate pride in his achieveents to the belief that he can achieve anything (the Tower of Babel syndrome). He is sometimes so overcome by his failures that he feels he can achieve nothing worth while. Man has not yet come of age. He is not mature, for he has not yet learnt how to cope either with his failure or with his success.

This book is about his failures, about his inadequacy and guilt. How does man in fact try to cope with them? How do the insights of Christianity suggest that he should cope with them? To these questions we now turn.

NOTES

1. London: Faber, 1948.
2. London: Cresset Press, 1956.

66

3. London: Secker and Warburg, 1948.

4. In *Oddly Enough*, London: Reinhardt, 1950. For later developments in resistentialist philosophy see *Even Oddlier*, London: Reinhardt 1952.

5. London: Secker and Warburg, 1956.

6. London: Weidenfeld and Nicolson, 1960.

7. London: Jonathan Cape, 1962.

8. London: Secker and Warburg, 1966.

9. London: Gollancz, 1954.

10. Deut. 13.

11. London: Hamish Hamilton, 1957.

12. *The Plague*, London: Hamish Hamilton, 1948.

13. Ps. 8.5.

14. Gen. 6.5.

15. Ps. 51.5.

16. Jer. 17.9.

4 Forgiveness and Community

So much for the problem: what of the solutions?

I have shown, I hope, that the problems of human guilt and inadequacy are real problems, and that they are felt to be real problems by many people today, and that whether one is a Christian or not a case can be made out for saying that the traditional Christian statement of the problems answers reasonably well to the facts. Can the same be said of the traditional Christian answers? Granted that Christian talk about guilt makes a certain amount of sense, does Christian talk about atonement make equal sense?

Many of the traditional answers are expressed in picturesque language, or in terms which we can only call mythological. They speak of Christ descending into hell, battling with the devil, or paying to God the price of man's ransom. Or they are expressed in terms of religious and social institutions which are no longer operative. They talk of Christ's death as a sacrifice, or they speak of his redeeming men from slavery, or they talk of atonement in terms of the satisfaction of God's honour, as if he were a mediaeval baron or a Germanic tribal chief.

We have two sorts of difficulties with explanations of this type. The fact that some are expressed in terms of defunct institutions means that to understand them requires a considerable imaginative effort. And even when the effort has been made successfully the explanation does not possess the immediacy or impact of one framed in terms of institutions of which we have first-hand experience. I can imagine what redemption meant to a slave, but I have never been a slave, or even met one.

In some cases the imaginative effort needed is great. In order to understand the mediaeval theories framed in terms of the satisfaction of God's honour, we not only need to comprehend mediaeval social institutions but to take a sympathetic view of mediaeval moral values. And in order to see the force of explanations which speak of Christ being *punished* on our behalf, we have to view sympathetically a way of thinking which to most of us is morally repugnant, since we find it hard to conceive of a divine justice which could require the deliberate punishment of the innocent.

But if these were the only difficulties, they would not be insuperable. All we should have to do would be to find an analogy framed in terms of living institutions and which made sense in twentieth-century conditions. In a later chapter I shall suggest some analogies which might be suitable for this purpose, but for the present I want us to face another difficulty which some of us have with the traditional expositions of the atonement. Our problem is not that they use unconvincing analogies, but the fact that they are analogies at all. An analogy, a mere parable or parallel, does not help us. We constantly feel the need to get back behind the analogy to the thing it signifies. What is it an analogy *of*?

When we read the textbooks of Christian dogmatics we find that they catalogue the traditional theories, point out the weaknesses of each of them, and usually end by saying that each presents the atonement from one, legitimate angle, but that a rounded doctrine of the work of Christ must take account of all of them. This is rather like being told that we cannot be allowed to see the thing we are searching for, but that instead we may be allowed a glimpse of it in a series of distorting mirrors, leaving to our imagination what the object looks like that could produce such an array of reflexions.

Now we must be prepared for the possibility that the atonement is an object of such curious properties that it cannot be looked at by any other means. But let us at least make the attempt. Let us *try* to dispense with analogies and see how far we get. Let us dispense, at any rate, with what look like the contrived analogies of Christian tradition; let us dispense, at least for the time being, with all picturesque and mythological language (we may well be obliged to come back to it later); and let us see what practical solutions to the problem of guilt human beings actually resort to.

Forgiveness and family

Guilt and failure are things which nearly all of us experience some of the time, and some of us experience nearly all the time. We have to live with them. How do we in fact make this unpleasant experience bearable for ourselves?

Guilt and failure raise problems first of all within human relationships. How do we deal with them in that context? Let us again begin by leaving God out of the question for a while. When we offend *each other*, when we let *each other* down, what do we do to assuage our guilty feelings, or to repair the damage we have done?

We cannot live intimately with one another, as in a family, or work closely with one another, without conflict. We have different ways of doing things, different priorities about what ought to be done. We all have qualities which irritate our fellows. The consequence is conflict, which is not in itself necessarily bad. Where there is no conflict, is there genuine encounter?

But one consequence of conflict is that sometimes we offend each other, upset each other, hurt each other. However harmonious a family, a friendship or a working partnership may be, there are moments or periods of disharmony. But we manage for most of the time to avoid disharmony, and we manage to overcome it when it does occur, by coming to terms with each other's weaknesses. And we do this, for the most part, with goodwill.

Perhaps the points I want to make will be clearer if we confine our attentions to one model, the family. If there is disharmony on the tennis club committee one can always resign from the committee or join another club. If one cannot get on with one's colleagues running the Boy Scouts, one can try to find a niche in the Youth Club. But if relations in the family are disturbed we cannot simply run away from the problem. We really do have to face it and come to terms with each other. And I say that for the most part we do it with goodwill.

70

One sometimes hears it stated that forgiveness is hard. It is easier to harbour resentment. But surely it all depends on who the offender is? If it is someone we love, a brother or sister, wife or husband, forgiveness is not an effort but a natural response. In the story of the Prodigal Son, *reason* may be on the side of the elder brother, but all our *sympathies* are with the father. How else could he act? After all, the prodigal was his son.

But within the family it is not just a matter of forgiving particular offences. Family life is only possible by an act. or an attitude, of continuing forgiveness. One does not simply forgive each day what grieves one, but forgives, as it were, in advance, the things one knows will grieve, and go on grieving. This is not, for the most part, done consciously; it is an underlying attitude. And the forgiveness is not only possible, but grateful, because it is reciprocal. The husband happily forgives the things that irritate or distress him about his wife, because he knows very well that she could only go on living with him if she were prepared to do the same for him. It is not only a matter of forgiving what we *do*. Some of us can only be lived with by people who are prepared to forgive what we *are*. They accept us, knowing that there are certain things about us which we regret but cannot help, and certain things about us which we do not regret and cannot even see are wrong.

I am not talking about tolerance. There is a difference between tolerating someone's weaknesses and actually accepting them, forgiving them. There is a sense in which weaknesses accepted and forgiven make a relationship stronger, whereas weaknesses tolerated only put an additional strain on it. Tolerance is only resentment mastered, and mastery of resentment is uncertain at best. The only real possibilities are either to go on forgiving what we do to each other or to go on resenting it.

Each of us needs a relationship as secure as this. In the long run life is only possible if there is someone, or some people, who accept us as we are. Much modern therapy depends on this fact. The depressive, the alcoholic, the drug addict, the delinquent, whatever else they need to rehabilitate them, need somewhere to belong, a community, or a group, or an individual friend, who will accept them, be concerned for them, and above all, not condemn them.

It may look like a paradox, but it is an indisputable fact of human nature, that if a personality is disintegrating it is only when he finds people who do *not* criticize his behaviour that he can find the strength of will to do something about it. When a man has sunk to the depths of failure or depravity it is no good urging him to pull himself out. It is no good telling him that everyone will rally round and help him once he is prepared to behave like a normal human being again. What he needs is someone who will care for him in spite of the failure and depravity, someone who will accept him, not after he has pulled himself out but while he is still in. If a man is an alcoholic it is no use his wife telling him that she will love him again if he will come off the bottle. There is a chance, however, just a chance, that he will find the strength to give up the bottle if she can convince him that she still loves him and will continue to love him *even if he fails.*

These are extreme examples, but the same factors are at work among those of us who are normal. Man can cope with his guilt, his failure and his inadequacy as long as he retains his self-respect. And he can only retain his self-respect if his community allows, if there is a community where he is respected. For most of us this community is the family, though it need not be. The family is the very community in which our short-comings are most obvious. Our wives, our husbands, our children or our parents are the very people best acquainted with them. They see us at our worst. It is the close and demanding relationships within the family that expose our weaknesses most ruthlessly. And yet here, where we ourselves are made most conscious of our failings, are the people who most willingly accept us as we are. Because they are prepared to come to terms with our failings, we can too. Properly appreciated, this knowledge does not make us complacent, only secure.

Forgiving one's self

In what way, precisely, does the accepting community or the

72

friend enable us to manage our feelings of guilt and inadequacy? Certainly not by disguising them or by minimizing them. I have said that the family provides just that situation which most ruthlessly exposes our weaknesses, and the same is true of any community which is intimate enough to give us the support I am talking about. True forgiveness does not pretend that the offence does not matter. It is within the family or other accepting community that we realize just how much it does matter, and become aware of what our shortcomings do to other people.

Neither does forgiveness pretend that the offence never happened. It accepts the offence as a fact, but refuses to allow it to disrupt the relationship. If forgiveness is genuine the relationship is certainly not weakened by it, and may even be strengthened.

Rarely, indeed, does forgiveness change the personality of the offender. It often has to be accepted that he is the sort of person who is likely to do the same again, and the person or community who forgives has got to accept that fact. To forgive someone is to accept him as he is, not to accept him conditionally. It is not to say, 'Well, we'll overlook it this time, but if it happens again . . .'. Only unconditional forgiveness can provide the security which a man needs in order to cope with his own failures.

What the offender has to learn from the forgiving community or the forgiving friend is to forgive himself. A man has to accept his guilt and his failure (in so far as they are real) and to come to terms with them on his own account. He has to come to terms with what he himself is. I say 'in so far as they are real' because there are certain unfortunate individuals whose chief need is to be told that their guilt feelings or their feelings of inferiority are founded on fantasy and that they are fretting themselves unnecessarily. But for the rest of us it is usually a matter of coming to terms with shortcomings which are all too genuine.

These things have to be faced positively. Simply to see oneself as a failure, or as a sinner, is debilitating and destroying. To face one's deficiencies positively is to see oneself as a failure or as a sinner and keep one's self-respect. And we cannot do this on our own. We can only do it for each other. The community or the friendship which accepts us in spite of our shortcomings enables us to accept ourselves, and to accept ourselves without illusions.

Christ as friend

Where does traditional Christianity fit in with the exposition of forgiveness which I have offered above? I have spoken of the importance of acceptance, of the necessity of belonging to a community which accepts us as we are, or of being in a relationship with someone who loves us as we are, and of the possibilities of self-forgiveness which then arise. What we have not so far noted is that such an experience can still provide stability, even if it is not an actual or existing experience. Some of us need the support of an intimate community or companion constantly, or we cannot face life. Some of us can survive great stresses in loneliness. Some can even stand alone against the opposition and contempt of their community, for a worth-while cause, and somehow meet the self-doubts that must powerfully arise in such a situation. A man may survive in such circumstances, not because he has a community or a friend on which to lean, *but because he had once*. His maturity of mind, his self-respect, his capacity to live with his guilt and doubts and failures have been formed by past experiences, past friendships, which continue to sustain him after they are ended.

This, of course, is why a stable childhood is so important. For most of us the archetypal person who accepts us, who continues to love us whatever we do and whatever we are, is the mother. It it is the formative relationship with our mother which gives us our emotional resilience. The effects of this relationship may last a lifetime, carrying us through awful miseries and humiliations, because here at least is one relationship in which we knew acceptance.

The sustaining relationship, therefore, may not be an existing or present one; it may be a past one. May it also be an ideal one? I have no doubt at all that for many Christians their faith in Christ works in just this way. They find their security in a relationship which supplies what their actual human relationships

74

lack, in a relationship with Christ. Christ is the one who knows all, and yet is prepared to forgive all. Christ is the partner and friend who cannot be offended and who loves in spite of all shortcomings. There is a sense in which, for any of us, no real human relationship supplies all the needed security. The mother-child relationship comes nearest to the ideal. For the normal child with the normal mother the security here is as absolute as it can humanly be. But this is a relationship which, vital as it is, the adult in some respects outgrows. Having grown out of childhood he knows very well that no human love is guaranteed to be bottomless. No human relationship is one-hundred-per-cent secure. But for the believer the love of Christ is bottomless. The love of Christ makes sense to his imagination because of his experience of human love. It is because he has known the love of a mother, of a family or a wife, that the love of Christ is conceivable to him, is real to his mind. But the love of Christ is like all these stripped of their imperfections.

None of this, of course, proves the reality of Christ. None of it goes even the smallest part of the way towards establishing the truth of Christianity. It would work just as well if Christ were a figure of the imagination. Though it would not work if he were *known* by the believer to be a figure of the imagination. But leaving open the question of whether it is true or not, there can be little doubt that this is part of the answer to the question of how Christianity actually achieves its results.

The other dimension of forgiveness

Is Christ, then, only a kind of psychological long-stop for those who find insufficient satisfaction in human relationships? Is he just a substitute friendly figure for those who cannot get on with their wives, their children or their fellow men? By no means! Belief in Christ adds another dimension both to our consciousness of guilt and failure and to our forgiveness.

In the light of Christ I see my guilt no longer as a small matter affecting my relations with my neighbour. It is no longer something which, however important it may be to me personally and to my immediate circle, stops there. In the light of Christ my guilt takes on a cosmic significance and an eternal one. And the forgiveness which I believe he offers takes on an equally momentous quality. In Christ I see my shortcomings not as mine only but as part of the huge weight of human dereliction, and I see them not merely as weaknesses, or as regrettable quirks in my nature, but as offences against Almighty God. And the forgiveness which is offered to me in Christ is God's forgiveness, and what takes place in me when I accept it does not affect me only. Somehow it is the sin and failure of the human race that is being dealt with here. This is where Christianity's attitude to guilt goes beyond that of the psychologist or any other purely secular attitude. It gives the whole phenomenon this other dimension, the cosmic and eternal one.

The desire for forgiveness, for reconciliation, for atonement, is one aspect of the universal human desire to change the past, to wish that things were otherwise, that certain events had not happened. Men have, to use a phrase, I think, of Tolkien's, 'an infinite capacity for regret'.

The Christian doctrine of reconciliation makes us, first, face up to the fact that the past cannot be changed. What's done is done. And what we have done is irrefutable evidence of what kind of people we are.

To be forgiven or reconciled does not, except in rare instances, in itself *change* the kind of people we are. This is most important to get straight. Christians make much of the power of the Holy Spirit to change lives, to make people different. It has been demonstrated over and over again that this can happen. Possibly it always *ought* to happen. But in fact it frequently does not happen, and the fact that it does not cannot be used as a criticism of Christianity. For if forgiveness is genuine it still stands, whether there is any change of character or not. The Christian is a man who has come to terms with his shortcomings, his guilt and his failure, first of all by seeing their magnitude, their cosmic and eternal significance, their nature as sins against God. And then by experiencing God's forgiveness, in Christ, of that sin. But there is no necessary reason why this coming to terms with his sin should make him less of a sinner or less of a failure.

It enables him to come to terms with sin and failure, to feel less guilty, less oppressed and incapacitated by weaknesses, but this is not at all the same thing as taking these unfortunate characteristics away. Certainly the Christian who properly appreciates the meaning of sin and forgiveness will try to overcome the shortcomings to which he is prone. If he really understands the hurt they do to his fellow man and to his God, he is bound to *want* to overcome them. But if forgiveness and reconciliation are to be worth anything, they must still hold, whether he succeeds or not.

Some will say: Isn't this a dangerous doctrine? Yes it is. I admit it. But if it is not true, then I for one must say that the gospel is no use to *me*. When a sinner is converted he will eventually, one hopes, become less sinful, but he does not stop being a sinner. He merely becomes a penitent sinner and a forgiven sinner.

What, then, is changed by the experience of reconciliation or acceptance? The past is not changed. The offender himself may not be. What is changed is some of the *results* of the past. What is changed is the significance of the past. You cannot undo, or only rarely, the practical consequences of past actions. But you can change what you let it do to you.

You cannot unsay what you said in a quarrel. To be truly reconciled is not to pretend that you didn't say it, nor to persuade each other that you didn't mean it. You have to begin by acknowledging that the hard things you said do express how you sometimes feel about each other. To be reconciled is to go on in honesty, each *knowing* how the other feels, and not allowing it to embitter the relationship. You have hurt, and been hurt. But what matters is what you let it do to you.

The Christian is a man who is not fettered by his past. He can look it squarely in the face and be neither resentful of it nor embittered by it nor disillusioned. 'Not disillusioned' is perhaps a misleading phrase. If someone is described as 'not *dis*-illusioned' it might by taken to mean that he is optimistic because he has his illusions still intact. But the Christian's cheerfulness is not founded on illusion. He does not sail on into the future in rash optimism about himself. He is of all men most realistic. But he is realistic without being cynical. He begins each day afresh, having written off the failures of yesterday. He knows they are there. He has faced them. He is penitent for them. But they no longer incommode him. This is what absolution means. The Christian knows he has failed, and knows he will fail again. And yet he is *free* of failure; free of its effects and free of its power.

This sense of freedom, of absolution, is something which can rarely be got from any human relationship. I may feel great security in a human relationship, be it with my wife, my analyst, my probation officer or my priest. I may feel completely confident that in that relationship I am accepted as I am, and that I will not be rejected because of anything I have done or may do. I may experience a great feeling of relief or freedom on the confession of some particular sin that has burdened me or on the clearing up of some particular misunderstanding or on the making up of a quarrel. But what that relationship is less able to give me is the feeling of being free of myself, of being right with the world, and right with God.

5   Drama, Ritual and Therapy

We have looked at some of the ways in which a community to which we belong, or even a single friend, can help us to come to terms with our feelings of guilt and failure. Let us now look at some other ways in which we try to do this.

We all have our problems. If they can be solved, well and good, but if not, then we must learn to live with them. If we cannot alter the problems we must alter ourselves, alter our attitude to them. If we cannot change the facts we must change ourselves to fit round them, or find them uncomfortable bedfellows.

The retreat into reality

One common way of coming to terms with our problems, which we all resort to sometimes, is by retreating into fantasy. We take flight into a world of the imagination where the facts are different and the problems do not exist. Some of this is probably necessary to our mental health, and certainly, if indulged in mildly, as most of us do, it seems harmless enough. When reading an escapist book or watching a gently romantic or adventurous film or play we are taking a little mental holiday. And perhaps we feel a little more refreshed to face life afterwards.

Films, books, magazines and television all help us to escape in this way into fantasy worlds. They transport us effectively, in imagination, into situations remote from our own, and allow us to identify ourselves with the characters portrayed, and to fancy ourselves brave, tough, romantic, or even tragic, as our inclination is, while the play or the book lasts.

But the magazines and the advertisments and the popular press do something more than this. They create another, apparently more real world, around the stars, the entertainers who *make* the plays and films. They help to create the illusion that there actually exists, on this earth, a world of glamour and glitter, inhabited by these beautiful people. The fact that it is also a world of wealth is almost incidental. And this world is made more attractive by the observation that fortunate people may break into it. 'Ordinary' girls and boys may be 'discovered', and become film stars or pop stars or television personalities. And some of these people are manifestly of quite modest abilities. So every hairdresser's assistant can plausibly dream to herself of entering the glamorous world, because entry to it, though remote, is possible.

But the more we think of our fantasies as real possibilities, the more dangerous they become. We may think of them as real possibilities which we have somehow missed. We may begin to feel that the world of our fantasy is a world which we really *deserve* to be admitted to, and which we ought to be enjoying, if it were not that cruel mischance or other people's failure to recognize our talents has deprived us of it. The person who thinks like this is likely to spend his life in sour contemplation of what he has missed.

Or we may think of our fantasy world as one which we may still inhabit, if we have the right lucky break. The possibilities are in this case real, but future. Fantasies of such a sort may be a spur to action, driving a man on to achieve his dream world. But in fact they rarely do work in this way. More frequently they act in the opposite fashion. Contemplation of the dream world becomes not a spur to action but a substitute for it. The dream world is a sort of mental dummy which we suck as a substitute for the real nourishment of success, an ineffectual comforter of our deprivation.

Or, most dangerous of all, we may think of the possibilities of our fantasies as real but present. We may credit ourselves with imaginary achievements and refuse to admit that reality is real. In the face of our inadequacy and failure we may erect round ourselves a vast wall of pretence. We pretend that we are a happy family after all. We pretend that we still love each other. We pretend that we still understand each other, still communicate.

We pretend we do not know how we really stand in the boss's estimation. We pretend that the firm thinks the world of us. We pretend that we are indispensable. The man who has got himself into this situation is done for if reality ever penetrates that wall.

The plays of Arthur Miller, and especially his overpowering *Death of a Salesman,* are as efficient and sensitive expositions of this theme as may be imagined. Miller probes human pretence in a way that is ruthlessly thorough and yet somehow sympathetic at the same time. He can expose a human being's immense capacity for self-deception so thoroughly that it shocks us, and yet so understandingly that we can never quite despise.

Getting it out of the system

Another way of coping with our problems is periodically to release the emotions they engender in us. This is easier in a crowd, and easier still if done in a licensed way. To yell support for our local football team in company with ten thousand or more other like-minded men has a cathartic and beneficial effect, especially if our side wins. And if they lose, further emotional release can be obtained by breaking up the football special, beating the wife or yelling at the kids.

The football match is an especially effective agent for the relief of emotion because of the element of conflict involved. Sport is a kind of ritualized combat. It is war, transferred from the battlefield to the arena. It provides relief for the aggressive instincts both of the participants and, by proxy, of the spectators. Sport becomes even more satisfying and effective as a discharger of violent emotions if it contains a real element of danger, if there is a real possibility of injury, or even death. This is one reason why motor racing will always have more crowd appeal than table tennis.

Sport is of immense importance in the modern world. It helps to maintain the health of society by getting rid in a harmless way of dangerous emotions and tensions. It is no accident that one of the oldest elements in religious ritual is the ritual combat. Men have always found some form of stylized combat

81

beneficial to their state of mind. The modern ritual combat of football, athletics or motor racing no longer has a religious setting, but there is little doubt that such spectacles fulfil for the spectators many of the needs that were met by the stylized combat in the religions of the ancient world.

Another common way of releasing emotion is in drunkenness. This is another 'licensed' situation. It is not that drunkenness is entirely approved of, but a drunken man can get away with behaviour which would not be tolerated in a sober one. The general attitude to drunkenness is ambivalent. In its milder forms it is smiled at rather than frowned on. In some sections of society it is regarded indulgently. In such quarters it may be accepted as the natural response both to misery and exuberance. A man is regarded as quite normal if he reacts to grief, or to depression, by 'drowning his sorrows'. But if he has just had a pay rise, or his wife has given birth to a baby, or the home team has won for a change, and he decides to 'celebrate', his behaviour will occasion just as little surprise. The end result, drunkenness, is in both cases the same, though the emotions which prompt it are entirely different. *Any* excess of emotion, of whatever sort, is felt to be a reason for getting drunk, because in drunkenness the emotion is provided with an outlet for vigorous, even violent expression. Whether one approves of this method of relieving tension or not, one has to grant it a measure of effectiveness. It may well be that the factory worker who regularly gets sozzled every Saturday and Sunday evening actually copes better with the grinding boredom of the rest of his working week because of it.

I hasten to add, for the benefit of all those friends of mine who are much better Methodists than I am, and by whom I do not wish to be misunderstood, that I am not *advocating* this way of relieving boredom or tension. I can think of better ones. I am merely pointing out that people resort to it only because it actually does work.

Some of the methods I have mentioned help us to deal with our problems by temporarily forgetting them, taking a little holiday from them. This is obviously not a lasting solution. It is not a positive solution, it only earns us a respite. But there are ways in which we can gain an element of relief and yet at the same time make some positive progress, if not towards the solution, at least towards the definition, of our dilemmas.

Ritual and catharsis

In the last section I perhaps too readily identified modern sporting contests and ancient ritual combat. There is one serious difference, and it is probably quite crucial. The ancient watcher of a religious ritual combat and the modern football spectator may not differ much in the level of their emotional involvement. They certainly differ in the significance which they attach to the conflict. The football spectator is watching Rovers play United, and what is at stake is a couple of notches up or down the league table, or even the cup. This issue may loom large enough in the eyes of the dedicated supporter, but even he would admit that defeat or relegation for his fancied team is not the end of the world. What the ancient spectator is watching, however, is the struggle between the forces of light and the forces of darkness. What is at issue is the fertility of next year's crops, the security of the throne, the whole order of nature and society. The wrong result *might* be the end of the world.

What the ritual is doing for the ancient observer is focusing the whole problem of his life; his struggle, and the struggle of his people, with the forces of infertility and chaos, with famine, drought and pestilence, with subversion and disorder, battle, murder and sudden death. For the ancient religious man the ritual gives shape, meaning, significance to his problems, his worries, his sense of individual and corporate inadequacy, his fears and feelings of the uncertainty of life. And for such a man religious ritual not only expresses and sums up what he feels about his predicament, but actually accomplishes something. It does not *solve* the problems of his existence, but by giving shape and definition to them, and by expressing and releasing the emotions which they engender in him, it enables him to cope with them or to live with them more satisfactorily and successfully.

83

Before going further it will perhaps be of value to digress a little to consider the part played by ritual in the modern world. Outside the sphere of religion we at first sight appear to make little use of it, but closer examination shows that it does survive, and survives strongly, in certain contexts. There are particular spheres of activity which have well-developed rituals of their own. There is the ritual of the law court, the ritual of parliament, the ritual of the state occasion, military ritual. Within their own spheres some of these rituals are treated very seriously indeed. International crises of quite grave proportions can be precipitated by failure to observe the rules of diplomatic protocol. Every kind of social activity has got its proper rules of conduct – in other words, its rituals. There are the rituals of the dance floor, the rituals of the business meeting (you address the chair, move and second propositions and amendments, propose votes of thanks, etc.). There are the ever present rituals of good manners.

Most of these rules are in a sense arbitrary, and recognized by those who use them to be arbitrary. But they are adhered to for the sake of good order. If they are recognized by everyone as the proper ways of doing things, then everyone knows what is happening and how to behave. It is very useful that all business meetings should be conducted according to much the same formulae, whether they be meetings of the Church Council, the Masonic Lodge, the Business Women's Luncheon Club or the board of directors of ICI. We do not attribute any occult significance to these rituals, but rituals they are, and they are socially important. They act as a kind of social cement, binding the members of society together in a common culture.

But rituals may be important for individual reasons, too. We need a certain amount of ritual not merely to preserve social order but to preserve order in our own lives. Extreme cases are often the most instructive. An old lady, living now alone, continues religiously to wash on Mondays and iron on Wednesdays. She rises unfailingly at seven a.m., whether she feels like it or not, and makes a cup of tea, just as she used to do for her husband. She has lunch every day at half-past twelve. Why? Her ritual is a link with the ordered world and with the ordered past, and with a society which she hardly any longer sees. She is not being foolish. When she stops washing on Mondays she will probably stop washing altogether. She will become dirty and will lose her reason. It is her ritual that is holding her personality together, and her self-respect.

We need to see an order in our existence, not only for the sake of efficiency but for the sake of sanity. And one way of imposing order is through ritual. These rituals are nearly always derived from our society. They are social rules. They are what all men do in the same circumstances. Private rituals are almost a contradiction in terms, but not quite. In extreme circumstances, when the personality is threatened with disintegration, even private rituals may be useful for holding it together, like the private rituals of the solipsist characters in Samuel Beckett novels.

I hope I have shown that for all of us, even in ordinary circumstances, rituals are more important than they may appear to be at first sight. But there are particular situations where they become more important still. There are particular moments in the lives of all men which are emotionally very highly charged. The experiences of marriage and of bereavement are perhaps the most obvious, though not the only ones. It is significant not only that societies of all sorts have commonly hedged round these experiences with ritual, but that the rituals associated with them have survived, and survived strongly, into modern times. Even the most rationalistic and hard-headed of twentieth-century Englishmen feels the need to mark with some sort of ceremony the great experiences of life. You *can* get married by saying a couple of sentences before two witnesses in a registry office, sign the register and go home on a bus. But not many people do. They generally, even if they do it in a registry office, prefer to declare the same by the giving and receiving of a ring, and by joining of hands, and by speech-making, toast-drinking and a very great deal of other palaver besides.

You *can* bury your mother by dropping her into a hole in

the ground, without so much as a prayer. But most of us don't. Even the unbeliever at such times likes to see earth sprinkled on the coffin and hear solemn words about 'ashes to ashes, dust to dust'. When it comes to expressing our deepest emotions and especially our corporate emotions, we often, still, resort to picturesque ceremonies and symbolic actions and words hallowed by generations.

The use of ritual at such times answers to a human need. The ritual acts as a sort of emotional lightning conductor. When faced with these stressful and highly charged situations, a man follows the established ritual procedures, and is comforted by them. The experience is unknown and frightening to him, but he knows that it is part of the common human lot. His fellows have been through it before him. So he is comforted by acting as his fellows have acted, and as his fathers have acted. He does what is expected of him, and the ritual imposes a pattern, and therefore a degree of understanding and acceptability, on a situation which is frightening and might become intolerably so.

Ritual removes the terror from the unknown by reminding a man that it is unknown only to *him*, the individual. To his race it is already ancient and familiar. So the ritual imparts to him an archetypal character. He takes on an archetypal role. At his high moment he is no longer a man, but Man, doing what Man has always done. This man and this woman before the alter take on the character of Adam and Eve, fulfilling the purposes for which matrimony was ordained. Their love is the archetypal love of Christ for his church. It is not accident that this symbolism finds its way into the marriage service. This is what ritual is all about.

The rituals of modern life are for the most part impoverished affairs, that have lost most of their power to move or to bind us. But they are not yet dead, and our need for them is not dead. Since the decay of religion our rituals, such as they are, have been fragmented. There is nothing to hold them together. There was a time when any solemn occasion was a religious occasion. If solemn words and symbolic acts were needed the materials lay ready to hand, in religious tradition. At the older British

86

universities degrees are still conferred in the name of the Father and of the Son and of the Holy Ghost. A blasphemous and hypocritical procedure, no doubt, but one which, at the time when these ceremonies were composed, seemed natural and right. At a modern secular university the equivalent ceremony cannot be religious. Yet a ceremony there must be. The resulting synthetic rituals have as much solemnity and significance as a game of ludo.

The point I am making is this, that though the rituals have lost their force, or much of it, the need which they exist to serve is still there. The graduand at the modern university *wants* his ceremony, though he mocks at it and feels cheated when he gets it. We *need* something to mark our solemn occasions; we need *rites de passage*. And the needs are still met, but piecemeal, and in unsatisfactory ways.

Ritual is not an endearing anachronism in modern society. It is not an optional extra, for those who are antiquated enough to like that sort of thing. It is not an irrelevance in a rationalistic society. To both society and the individual a ritual pattern, a coherent ritual pattern, is in the long run a necessity. By its means we deal with the traumatic experiences of life. We impose shape, order, meaning on experience.

The sense in symbols

Let me briefly digress a little further, and move on from ritual to symbolism. Man, even rationalistic, no-nonsense twentieth-century man, has a tremendous capacity, and indeed appetite, for symbolic actions. Take, for example, the flag. People have a passionate attachment to flags. People will die for flags. To burn a flag, to trample on a flag, is a very serious action. Why is it illegal to fly an Irish tricolour in Belfast? Why make a law against the display of a simple, harmless piece of cloth?

One reason is that symbolic action is a form of communication, and it may communicate more dramatically and potently than other forms of language. The American youngsters called up to serve in Vietnam made a more effective protest by burning their draft cards than any number of defiant words would have done. The Olympic athletes who wore a black glove each on the winners' rostrum were expressing their feelings more pointedly than by any speeches at a press conference.

But this cannot be the whole answer. Not all symbolism is communication. It cost no one knows how many hundreds of thousands of dollars per ounce to land a pay-load on the moon. It cost no one knows how many hundreds of thousands of dollars a second to keep men there. It was surely madness for any of those precious ounces or precious seconds to be wasted. Yet how many of both were spent in erecting a flag, and in depositing medals, and pious messages which no sentient being will ever see? If symbolism is language, this is man speaking to no one but himself.

Some would describe the whole expensive exercise of the moon landings as undertaken largely for symbolic reasons, as an expression of man's own self-confidence, as a demonstration of American superiority, as part of man's age-old romantic quest to reach the stars.

Do not dare, O gentle, agnostic reader, to dismiss any religious act as *merely* symbolic. Most human activities are undertaken for no better reason.

End of digression, and conclusion from it: if man needs ritual, and symbolic actions generally, in order to impose a pattern on his experience, to give meaning to his existence and to help him to live with his dilemmas, and if the rituals and symbols of modern life do not help him as much as they might, what other methods are there at his disposal for achieving the same ends?

Therapeutic drama

I have spoken already of the kind of films, plays and other entertainments which we call 'escapist' and of the way in which they help us to deal with our problems by temporarily forgetting them. This is obviously not a lasting solution. But neither is it the only way in which these various entertainments can help us to cope with life. They can sometimes help us in other ways than merely assisting us to relax.

A good drama (and I am using the word 'drama' very broadly, to include films, television, live theatre, opera, ballet and even simple reading) invites us into a world of the imagination, a different world. It is always in one sense an unreal world, and yet by entering it we are not necessarily escaping from the world around us. From this world of the imagination we may actually see our real problems more clearly. By putting ourselves into the shoes of the characters in the play or book or whatever (and if it is a good drama we do this instinctively, we 'identify', as the saying is) we learn something about ourselves. We feel with the characters. We feel sorry for them or pleased for them. We understand why they act the way they do, and why, being themselves, they could not act otherwise. And in understanding them we understand ourselves better, and we understand our children or our colleagues or our wives better.

And there is more to it even than this. Good drama is not merely instructive. Perhaps it is not even primarily instructive. But in clarifying our problems it actually seems to accomplish something. This does not mean that it brings us any nearer to a practical solution to our dilemmas, but it puts them in a different perspective. They fall into place a little more. Without changing the problems at all, the drama can change our attitude to them and our outlook on them. It can give our lives a different and a more satisfying meaning. It can impart significance.

The world into which the drama transports us may bear little or no immediate resemblance to the actual world. It may be a world of pure fantasy. And yet while we are in it, that world appears to be in some senses more real than our own.

Drama in the modern age may meet some of the needs that modern ritual largely fails to meet. Drama and ritual are closely allied, and in the ancient world were indistinguishable. Ancient man acted out his concerns, his phobias, his dilemmas and his understandings, his insights and his intuitive grasp of what life was about. He not only acted them out, he put them into his stories, into his myths and sagas and legends. He put them into his histories. And we do the same. The only difference is that we have more media of communication at our disposal.

Two features of dramatic experience are worth noting. First, it is more potent when shared. Dramatic experience at its most effective is communal experience. This is perhaps one reason why, though television may have the advantage in the field of escapism, when it comes to more serious drama the live theatre has the edge. In the live theatre the actor can respond to the audience and the audience to him. Stage and auditorium can interact. There is more to the sharing of the dramatic experience than simply laughing together at the funny bits and experiencing the same emotions while sitting in adjacent seats. In the best drama the audience feels involved, it feels as if it is part of the action. And in religious ritual the congregation really *is* part of the action.

Second, though drama in the modern age uses media of communication which were unknown to our ancestors, the content of what is communicated is surprisingly constant throughout human history. In particular, there are certain themes and images which recur in stories, rituals and plays from time immemorial right down to the present. Really powerful drama is often powerful, not simply because it is technically well constructed, poetically expressed or expertly put across, but because it makes skilful use of variations on these primordial themes. Such themes, and the images and symbols in which they are expressed, are like keys which fit the various locks of universal human experience. Or they are like chords which are in tune with the natural resonances of our souls, with which we can vibrate in harmony. They touch something profound in us, and bring out patterns in our experience which men have always felt to be peculiarly satisfying and meaningful, the tragic and the comic rhythms of birth, passion and death.

Drama and story bring out the significance of existence, but not in a way that is merely intellectually satisfying. They are emotionally satisfying, too, and at the same time somehow productive. They help man actually to manage his experiences better, to cope with his tensions, his unfulfilled and unfulfillable hopes, his aggressions, his gnawing frustrations, his sense of failure and of guilt, and also to express his delight, his joy in living, his satisfactions, his desires, his love.

I have probably made it sound as if I am talking only about serious drama, or should I say Serious Drama? I am not. If the satisfactions I have indicated above were available only to the watchers and readers of Pinter, Becket, Ionesco and Brecht, or even of Shakespeare, the phenomenon of drama would not be of widespread significance. On my definition of the word *Softly, Softly* is drama, cowboy films are drama, *Tom and Jerry* is drama. A very large number of people in western society spend a large part of their lesiure time watching drama. Why do they find it so satisfying? Some of it is escapism, but by no means all. The three examples I have mentioned above may well contain escapist elements, but they certainly exhibit the ancient mythic themes as well. I shall not analyse the examples in great detail. The reader is invited to try it for himself. But I shall suggest the sort of lines on which I think they may be analysed.

When people discuss violence on television they never seem to quote the Tom and Jerry cartoon. Yet it is easily the most violent among current regular programmes. The theme of ritual combat is central. The fact that it is *ritual* combat is clear. No one ever gets permanently hurt (in spite of the most astonishing and vicious treatment which the combatants deal out to each other). And if ever it looks as if real damage has been done, the opponent is always overcome with remorse. The conflict is also archetypal. The conflict of cat and mouse is universal, cosmic, in the nature of things. Individual cats catch individual mice, but the archetypal, cosmic cat (Tom) chases the eternal mouse (Jerry) down all the ages from the beginning of time into eternity. To the male viewer (the programme has much less appeal to women) the violence itself is deeply satisfying. And there is another ancient mythic motif which appears in the mouse's evident superiority of intelligence. This is the 'success of the underdog' motif which abounds in myths and legends.

Perhaps it would be true to say that whereas intellectual drama (the Pinter, Becket, Ionesco sort) succeeds by cleverly disguising its mythic themes and patterns, popular drama succeeds very often by throwing them into relief, by stereotyping them.

The cowboy film, or western, illustrates this very well. There are thousands of westerns, but only one story. This story is apocalyptic in its simplicity, and monotonously predictable in its outworking. But it is exactly in this simplicity and predictability that the appeal of the western lies. We know what is going to happen. We should feel intensely cheated if our expectations were not fulfilled. There are the goodies and the baddies, (the sons of light and the sons of darkness). The baddies outnumber the goodies. The baddies are richer, more powerful. Outrage is committed, or planned (bank robbery, robbery of stage coach, or, more potent mythic theme, dispossession of small landholder). The goodies are effectively reduced to one, the hero, possibly with very few assistants. In spite of the odds the hero challenges the forces of evil. There is the chase, the fist-fight, and the final showdown with guns. Good triumphs, the cosmic harmony is restored.

Again we have the ritual conflict, not this time the eternal but amoral conflict of cat and mouse, but a conflict between starkly contrasted good and evil. The morality of the western is simple, but utterly uncompromising. In the real world, of course, such absolute and clear moral alternatives are the exception. In the world of myth they are the norm. All men, and all courses of action, are in the world of myth either clearly good or clearly bad.

The typical western is not only good popular entertainment, it is a declaration of faith. It declares the conviction that however complicated life may look, there is a fundamental distinction between good and evil, and that though the forces of good may appear to be weaker, they will triumph in the end. It admits that life is turbulent and that conflict is intrinsic to it. It admits that to side with the good may be a heroic act, but asserts the necessity of that act. It is because they contain these assertions and these themes that westerns are so satisfying.

Crime stories are less stereotyped, but they lend themselves to a similar analysis. But perhaps the richest vein of contemporary popular fiction and drama is science fiction. I myself have hardly explored this domain at all, but I have seen enough of it to realize that in that realm of fantasy a manifold assortment of mythic themes and motifs has space to flourish. The world of science fiction is the fantasy world, the dream world, of the twentieth century, and I suspect that to the skilful analyst twentieth-century man exposes there more clearly than anywhere else the mysteries of his *psyche*. I suspect, too, that on analysis that world would turn out to be peopled by all the gods and demi-gods, heroes, titans, demons and monsters that have peopled men's imagination since the dawn of time, but all wearing space helmets.

What I am saying, then, is that drama and story, whether they are on the level of Arthur Miller or of Doctor Who, fulfil functions which are vital to our psychic well-being. Men have some deep psychic needs which traditionally they satisfied by means of religious rituals and enactments and stories. These needs are no longer met for most of us by religion, and have not been met exclusively by religion for many centuries. But the fundamental methods of meeting them are still the ones which religion has always used, only they have been 'desacralized' (horrible word, I think it was the anthropologists who invented that one). Man cannot do without his myths and his rituals, and in particular his ritual of combat and his myth of the triumph of good. Our ancestors presumably got their diet of rituals in the tribal assembly. They sang their myths round the tribal bonfire and danced them in the tribal dance. We get our diet on the sports field and from the telly.

It is still very difficult to describe how drama achieves its effects. And when we have watched a profound and satisfying drama we may often be quite unable to pin down just what has been said, just what answer is being offered for the human dilemma. Sometimes, indeed, it is very evident that no sort of answer is being offered, only another statement of the problem. But we nevertheless have the feeling, if the drama has been a successful one, that something has changed. Something has been *done*, something has fallen into place. There is an experience here that has something of the quality of revelation, the 'Ah! *Now* I see' quality. Good drama, successful myth, effective ritual, these carry their own conviction. They need no explanation, and indeed cannot be given one, in any terms other than their own. We may not be able to sum up their meaning in words that satisfy the rationalist in us, but on a different level of consciousness they make sense all right.

6   Death as Communication

We have looked at the profound significance which story, drama, and their component themes and images can have for us, and the functional value which they possess for us. With this behind us, let us examine the central image of the Christian religion, the image that appears in its most potent stories and most prominent rituals, and is central to its art and its theology, the image of the redeeming death of Christ.

Sacrifice

We shall not get very far without using the word sacrifice. It is primarily as a sacrifice that Christian tradition has always presented the death of Christ. And this is an especially potent interpretation of it because sacrifice has a long religious history of its own. It was already a powerful idea before Christianity ever came to make use of it. So let us begin by setting the record straight about sacrifice. I say 'setting the record straight' because a vast amount of nonsense has been written in books and talked in sermons about sacrifice. I may not know much about theology but I do know something about this.

Sacrifice is not a single phenomenon. It is a group of associated phenomena. It is not the expression of a single, simple idea. It has a number of roots. Different kinds of sacrifice, expressing different ideas and with different objects in view, may well have arisen spontaneously and independently and only later have been seen as variants of the same thing and have had the same label 'sacrifice' attached to them. By the time we reach the historical period, sacrifice in any given culture already has a rich complex of ideas gathered round it. In most cultures where sacrifice is practised it takes several forms.

And in each different form a different idea may be uppermost.

There is no rationale of sacrifice, no single explanation of how it works. There never was. Sometimes ancient man would talk in terms which seem to imply one or other theory or explanation of sacrifice, but we very frequently find the same man, or other men in the same cultural milieu, using alternative or contradictory explanations. The usefulness of sacrifice did not depend on any explanations with which it might be provided. It was regarded by almost everybody who made use of it as self-authenticating and self-explanatory.

The most obvious interpretation of sacrifice is to regard it as a gift, usually of food, to a deity. This explanation fits a wide range of sacrificial phenomena, but by no means all. Sometimes when ancient man offered a sacrifice he had no clear idea of whom it was offered to. It was not offered *to* anybody. It was simply offered. Neither does the gift explanation fit the not insignificant number of instances in which God himself was supposed to have provided the sacrifice. Furthermore, the gift explanation was exposed to an objection of which men from quite early times were well aware. The most familiar expression of this objection, to most of us, is in Ps. 50:

> For every beast of the forest is mine,
> the cattle on a thousand hills. . . .
> If I were hungry, I would not tell you;
> for the world and all that is in it is mine.

Sometimes it looks as if the notion of releasing life is the uppermost one, though I have never come across any passage in ancient literature which articulated this interpretation; it is a modern anthropological one. In sacrifices which lend themselves to this interpretation, the manipulation of the blood and its proper disposal is regarded as very important. Yet this explanation very evidently will not cover more than a fraction of sacrificial phenomena, for the vast majority of sacrifices which ancient man offered did not involve blood at all. They were offerings of cakes, bread, flour or other vegetable matter. It is very significant that Leviticus, after describing the ritual of the

96

guilt offering, in which the manipulation of the blood appears to be all-important, goes on to say that the sin offering, if a man is too poor to afford it, can be replaced, without loss of efficacy, by a handful of meal, which suggests that the manipulation of the blood cannot be all-important after all.[1]

In some instances sacrifice seems to be thought of as having some direct effect on sin and guilt. It seems to be conceived as in some fashion removing the stain or impurity which the offence brought on. It is very widely assumed by uninstructed Christians that this connexion with sin and guilt is the *sine qua non* of sacrifice. Sacrifices, they think, were always offered as expiations. This is just not true. Christians have seized on the phenomenon of expiatory sacrifice because it was this type of sacrifice which lent itself most readily to being used in the interpretation of the death of Christ. And it is also true that in the Jewish tradition, from which Christianity sprang, sacrifices for sin were very prominent. But even in Jewish tradition, expiatory sacrifice is by no means the only sort. Very many, and at some periods most, Jewish sacrifices were offered as thanksgivings, or in fulfilment of vows, or as expressions of rejoicing. Many sacrifices, both in Jewish and pagan tradition, had no evident connexion with sin.

Another favoured interpretation of sacrifice is that it is conceived as a meal, a meal shared with the deity, which thus brings men into fellowship with him. This, too, may look attractive. Some sacrifices in the ancient world were meals. Perhaps most of them were. But very many were not. There are a number of sacrifices in the Old Testament of which no part was eaten by the worshipper, and this type of sacrifice proves to be very ancient. It can be paralleled in many cultures. If ancient man were really thinking of his sacrifice as a meal shared with the god, it would have been very easy to devise a ritual which symbolized the idea. He might have set a place for his god at the table, for example. Yet examples of any such symbolism are extremely difficult to find.

Sacrifice is a phenomenon about which it is impossible to generalize. The only thing one can say about sacrifice, which would be true of all forms of it, is that it consists of offering. Yet it is virtually ubiquitous in the ancient world and in primitive cultures. Its appeal is universal, its explanation elusive. To ancient man it evidently meant a very great deal, and what it meant he regarded as self-explanatory. So when the early Christians described the death of Christ as a sacrifice, they were saying something that to them was very profound and meaningful. They were advancing a rich and many-sided explanation. To us it means very little. To us the institution of sacrifice itself cries out to be explained.

The way in which in modern English we use the word 'sacrifice' does not help to clarify the issue. Since we no longer need the word in religious contexts, it has been deprived of its religious meaning. 'His parents sacrificed to send him to university.' 'At some sacrifice to his dignity. . . .' 'If this church is to meet its financial commitments its members must give *sacrificially*' (in plain English, put five shillings in the collection plate instead of half-a-crown). But sacrifice in the ancient world was everywhere and always a religious act, and not necessarily a specially costly one. We might broadly classify the purposes for which it was undertaken into two principal kinds. These purposes are not mutually exclusive, but I think they can be logically distinguished.

First, it is a means of prevailing on God to do something, to forgive an offence, let us say, or to provide help. In some religious systems this may be quite depersonalized. The divinity to whom the sacrifice is presented may not be conceived in really personal terms. Sacrificial ritual in this case is close to magic. It is regarded as achieving its results in almost mechanical ways. Offering the sacrifice is rather like putting money in the slot. This is not, however, a common view, and emphatically not a biblical one. Most religions think of sacrifice as somehow prevailing on a personal deity.

Secondly, sacrifice expresses what the devotee feels. This may indeed be the way in which it is held to have its effect on the god. It may obtain the forgiveness or the help by demonstrating how badly the devotee needs it.

98

Voluntary death

My attempt to clarify the term 'sacrifice' has led the reader to see, I hope, how difficult a term it is to handle. The features of sacrifice which made it a useful concept to the first Christians, useful, that is, for conveying what they believed about the death of Christ, are the very features which make it less useful for doing the same job today. To them sacrifice was a living institution, which was understood in its own terms. And for a long time afterwards it was a still-remembered institution. But to us it is no longer alive or remembered. It does not speak to us in its own terms; it has to be explained in other terms. And the terms in which we most naturally explain it are highly misleading ones.

A concept which we do understand, and one which may be used very suggestively in our consideration of the meaning of the death of Christ, is that of voluntary death. Voluntary death is a phenomenon which is at once both wider and narrower than the ancient institution of sacrifice.

It is a narrower term in that a great deal of what is properly called sacrifice did not, as I have already pointed out, involve the death of anyone or anything. Moreover, the element of willingness in the victim is no part of the concept of sacrifice, as anciently understood. The willingness or unwillingness of the victim was not usually considered relevant to the business in hand. So the description 'voluntary death' leaves out a good deal which the term 'sacrifice' includes.

But likewise, 'voluntary death' includes quite a lot that the term 'sacrifice' leaves out. Sacrifice, as I have already argued, properly speaking covers only religious acts. Voluntary death may be, but need not be, a religious act. So there are many instances of voluntary death which cannot be called, in this accurate sense of the word, sacrificial.

No man will be prepared to die without good reason. What sort of reasons are conceivable? We might classify them in the same way as we classified the reasons for sacrifice; to achieve a specific result, or to express a feeling, i.e. as a gesture.

It is not difficult to think of circumstances in which men have died voluntarily in order to achieve specific ends. Such things happen in war, for example. The Japanese suicide bombers in the last war were really a species of guided missiles, guided by living men who knew that they would themselves be destroyed in the destruction they inflicted on the enemy. For reasons the westener finds it hard to understand, they were prepared to be regarded as part of the machinery and, like the machinery, expendable. A more sympathetic example to most of us is the famous one of Captain Oates, the member of Scott's ill-fated Antarctic expedition who crawled out into the night so as not to encumber his companions and to increase their chances of survival. Every reader will doubtless be able to think of examples of his own.

There are even more occasions when men will *risk* death for the sake of attaining a specific object. This can happen in some sorts of experimental work, for instance. One thinks of Humphrey Davy, deliberately letting the gas in his room reach the proportions of an explosive mixture, in order to test his newly-invented safety lamp.

A new dimension is added to heroism when, instead of risking possible death to achieve a certain end, a man accepts certain death to achieve an end that is no more than probable, and which he has no guarantee will be achieved. His life is offered simply in hope and in faith.

Let us turn now to the other possible reason for voluntary death, the expression of a feeling, an attitude, a point of view. This is a commoner phenomenon than might at first be imagined. Consider, first of all, the matter of suicide.

Suicide is characteristically seen in the west as 'the coward's way out'. It is regarded as a running away from the problems of life. It is committed by people in despair, who can no longer face the difficulties of living. Such a view ignores the fact that in cultures other than our own, both ancient and modern, suicide has often been viewed not as an escape, but as an honourable gesture, or as a dignified way of bowing out of an extreme situation. Not only so, but it ignores the real facts about suicide even in our own culture.

An examination of many actual instances shows that suicide is very frequently indeed a kind of appeal, an appeal for sympathy, an appeal for help. A woman may try suicide in an attempt to get across to some other person just how bad she really feels. It is an attempt to communicate in death something she failed to communicate in life. It is very easy to see such motivation behind that very common occurrence, the suicide attempt which is not meant to succeed. Such an 'attempt' is no more than a demonstration. But anyone who has looked closely at the phenomenon will confirm that the same motivation is often apparent behind serious and successful attempts. Very many suicide attempts to do not come clearly either into the category of mere demonstrations or of serious efforts. They are in effect hazards. They have a real chance of succeeding, and a real chance of being discovered before it is too late, and they are undertaken on that basis. If failure is the result, then 'Now they'll *have* to do something about me. At last they'll have to take me seriously.' If they succeed, then, 'At least they'll know how bad I felt. They'll *have* to understand. They'll see what they've done to me.' And perhaps sometimes the feeling is, 'Now they'll suffer as they've made me suffer.'

What this amounts to is that, whether in success or in failure, the suicide is often, perhaps even typically, an attempt to communicate. The method is chosen because it demonstrates just how desperate the need to communicate is. The serious or successful suicide expresses the fact that the need to communicate is so urgent that it must be accomplished even though one die in the doing of it.

There are other kinds of voluntary death which, though they are broadly to be classed as suicides, are not on the same level as the kind I have just been talking about, and some of us might be reluctant to use the word 'suicide' of them at all. They are not personal appeals for understanding, but gestures in support of a cause. But they are certainly attempts at communication. Emily Davidson, the suffragette who threw herself in front of the king's horse in the Derby, was asserting her belief in a cause. And by making her assertion in this form she demonstrated

101

the supreme importance she attached to it. No statement can be more urgent than this, that one is prepared to die in the making of it.

Death, therefore, can not only be a statement. For the person making it, it is the ultimate statement. It is the method of communication resorted to when all other methods have failed to obtain a response.

Edward Albee's *Zoo Story*² seems to be presenting, in another way, this same idea. It begins with an apparently casual conversation between two men, but it gradually dawns on us that one is trying deliberately to provoke the other. The provocation becomes sharper and more intense until it becomes clear that violence will be the result. Slowly it emerges that this is exactly what the assailant wants. He wants to be attacked. He is inviting this acquaintance to kill him. In the end, he does. And the assailant is happy. He has done what he set out to do. He has made the man *respond*.

If voluntary death is conceived as a gesture, what precisely can it accomplish? It is conceived as a communication, and sometimes the fact *that* it communicates is more important than *what* it communicates. It is intended to provoke a response, and the fact that it gets a response is almost more important than the nature of the response it gets. If we ask in precise terms what such a death accomplishes, the answer may be very hard to come by.

Early in 1969, shortly after the invasion of Czechoslovakia by the Russians, a young student, Jan Palach, set himself on fire in Wenceslas Square, Prague, and burnt to death. The effect of this on Czech feeling was extraordinary. The event may have struck many foreigners as pointless and futile, but Czechs of all kinds found it to be profoundly meaningful. It summed up, better than anything else at the time, how they felt. It expressed despair, that the Czech bid for freedom had come to an end, and yet faith in the value of what they had attempted. It was an expression of impotence. This is what we have come to, all we have left, to die. Both the youth of Jan Palach and the manner of his death were profoundly moving.

102

The death of Jan Palach is difficult to justify rationally. It made its appeal direct to the imagination. It was a powerful statement, both of faith and of despair. But its practical effects would be very difficult to determine. In the long run perhaps they are not very impressive. But its object was presumably not to *do* anything at all, for it seemed to be an acknowledgement that there was nothing to be done. A gesture was all that remained. But it was not a *mere* gesture. It was, and remains, an assertion of the value set by Jan Palach and his fellow countrymen on the things for which he died: on democracy, on humanity, on 'socialism with a human face'.

In the loose sense we might call Palach's death sacrificial, but it was not a religious act. Jan Palach's life was not offered *to* anything or anybody. It was offered *for* something: for Czech freedom and Czech nationhood. It was not an attempt to accomplish anything. It was to express something, a mood, a feeling, a judgment on a situation. And as such it must be judged.

I want here to refer back to Arthur Miller's play, *All My Sons*, which I mentioned earlier,[3] for it includes a good example of a voluntary death which does accomplish something, though possibly not all that it set out to do. The deliberate death of Joe's airman son was presumably intended to do something to Joe. It was an expression of what the son felt about his father's behaviour, and would have remained so, even if Joe had never found out about it. But Joe *was* meant to find out about it. It was an attempt to communicate with him and to make him respond. Up to a point is succeeds. It does change Joe's perspective. It does let him see at last what he has done. The death of the son does succeed in doing what everybody else has failed to do. It 'gets through' to Joe.

But Joe's response gets stuck half way. The death brings Joe to the point of remorse, but no further. If he could have accepted the son's death as in some sense an expiation for his own sin, and with his changed perspective and new self-knowledge had decided to go on living, then the analogy with sacrifice would have been a very close one. The son's death, rightly apprehended,

103

might have had very real moral effects on the living, a point which the film of *All My Sons* tried to bring out, as the stage play does not (if I am remembering the film rightly – it is nearly twenty years since I saw it).

So here we have an example, fictitious but credible, of a voluntary death which did accomplish something and conceivably could have accomplished more. How are the effects achieved? They are achieved solely by affecting the emotions and imagination of others. If a death is intended to communicate, it must be made known to other people or it fails entirely. And if they, in spite of the urgency of the attempt, fail to respond, or if they misunderstand and respond in the wrong way, then the attempt fails, the death is futile. The effectiveness of the death depends on whether, and how, people react to it. This is an important point to bear in mind when we come to consider the bearing of what we have learnt from our study of voluntary death upon our understanding of the death of Christ.

The significance of a death depends partly on the manner of it, partly on the reasons known to lie behind it, i.e. on the *intention* of the one who dies, and partly on his *character*. The first two of these observations perhaps need no expansion, but something more needs to be said about the third. One may concieve of circumstances in which a heroic or self-sacrificing act may appear to bear no relation to the character of the one who makes it, in which, so to speak, the life suddenly takes on a virtuous character by the fact of its being offered. An example which springs to mind is Bret Harte's story of the gambler, a man with no previous record of altruism and of few known virtues, but who, when stranded with several companions, without any heroics of demonstration of emotion, sacrifices his own life for theirs.[4]

Generally speaking, however, the significance of a death depends as much on the manner of living as on the manner of dying. Certainly there is additional potency and significance in a death when a man dies for what he has lived for. Death encountered for the sake of a cause, for a reason, becomes in itself an achievement. The death of Martin Luther King was not, in the plain sense of the term, a voluntary death. It was not deliberately sought, though it was deliberately risked. Martin Luther King knew it was always a possibility, and perhaps, in the long run, even inevitable. He was not the first, and may well not be the last civil rights leader to die in the USA, but his death had an impact which few other deaths in our generation have had. It communicated something, not because of what it was in itself, but because it was part and parcel of the life and character of the man. His death took its significance from what he was and what he did when living.

Have I established the fact, then, that death may be, at least in some few instances, a form of communication? It draws its power from the fact that it is a once-for-all statement. The man who makes it cannot make it again. Neither can he again make any other statement. It is thus an assertion of the supreme and unique importance in his eyes of the thing for which he dies.

It is intended to evoke a response. This response may be a form of action or it may not. The death may be meant simply to make us think, or to make us feel, or to let us know how things are. It may be a statement of faith. It can convey a range and mixture of emotions such as it would be difficult to put into words, and convey them with an intensity which words could possibly never convey.

But I think there is another reason why such signs are effective. They appeal to something atavistic and deep rooted in the human mind. The sacrificial death is an ancient and almost ubiquitous theme of religion and folklore, myth and legend. Over and over again we encounter tales, and rituals, which are centred on the one who allows himself to be killed in order to bring benefit to mankind. From what recesses of the human spirit this idea springs, and whence it draws its power to move the imagination, I do not know. But I suspect that real examples of voluntary death make their impact partly because they draw on the power of this archetype.[5]

The death of Christ

I mentioned earlier some of the traditional interpretations of the death of Christ, as a sacrifice, as a ransom, as a punishment, and indicated briefly some of the all too obvious drawbacks which they have for ourselves.[6] I repeat once more that I do not wish to dismiss these interpretations as valueless or meaningless. They have been found helpful by generations of Christians. They are still found helpful by Christians today. Any of us may find the significance and value of them if he is prepared to consider them sympathetically and ask what it is that they are really trying to say. The fact remains that it requires an initial effort on our part. We have serious difficulties to get over before we begin, difficulties which I have already hinted at.

To see the death of Christ as a communication may be a little easier for twentieth-century man. We all know what communication is, and how important it is, and how difficult it can sometimes be. The need to understand each other, and the urgency of that need, is apparent to us all. We constantly feel that we are speaking different languages from each other, starting from widely different points of view, making radically different assumptions from each other. Workers and manage-, ment make the same complaint of each other, dons and students, parents and children: we are not speaking the same language. And all too often one side or the other feels that the only way to break down the barrier to communication is by violence. Not until there is a resort to violence does the opposing side see what the complaints are about or how strong the feelings are. Not until there is violence does the party in authority take the views of the underprivileged seriously. We are all familiar with this situation. To present the death of Christ therefore, as the one violent act which tries to initiate or restore communication has the merit of making it, at least at the start, comprehensible. This approach, like all others, has its difficulties, but before we look at them, let us examine a little more closely the idea of the death of Christ as an attempt to communicate.

First, it must be made clear that this is no new approach to the significance of the death of Christ; it is a variant of an old one. It is a variant of the interpretation put forward by the mediaeval scholar Peter Abelard.[7] Abelard did not reject the traditional theories of the atonement.[8] His interpretation is not a thoroughgoing replacement of the existing and accepted ones. It seems to have been conceived rather as an addition to them. This is an important fact to bear in mind when evaluating Abelard's contribution to the discussion. Abelard sees the death of Christ as an appeal, God's appeal to men. God offered his son, allowed him to die in this way, in order that we might appreciate how much he loved us. Christ's death is a demonstration of the love of God and the lengths to which it will go. It 'works' by moving men to love him in return. When they see the depth of his love they cannot but respond. They repent of their sins and turn away from them.

Abelard's suggestion offers a readily understood explanation of how the death of Christ achieves its effects on men. According to Abelard, it no longer needs to be understood as a legal or quasi-legal transaction between superhuman powers. It achieves its ends by the palpable effects which it has on the emotions and the minds of men.

In presenting Christ's death as a communication, therefore, or as an appeal, I begin where Abelard began. This approach is more acceptable to our modern outlook because it seems to take the matter off the mythological level. It is no longer a mysterious piece of business between God and the devil, or a transaction between God, man and Christ relating to sin, or honour, or punishment. It is Jesus's statement. It is the statement of a certain set of values, the values for which and by which he lived. It is a statement of the supreme importance of those values, that he will die rather than compromise them, die in order to express them. Jesus came to force men to respond. They did; some by killing him; some by attaching themselves to him, living for what he had lived for, and in some cases dying as he had died. Jesus had no guarantee that the appeal he made in dying would be understood or heeded. He had no guarantee that anything he had stood for would survive his death. His death is a statement of faith, and a statement made in faith.

The story of the death of Christ still makes its appeal, after all these years. It is still a potent appeal. Here we come back to what I said about the importance of drama and of story in our lives. In the story of Christ, recounted and enacted again and again in the rituals of the church, we have an immensly powerful drama. When we appropriate what it has to say to us we find it deeply satisfying. It helps us to make sense of existence. It puts our dilemmas and achievements both into perspective. It convinces us about what things are, after all, most worth living for and most worth dying for. It appeals, as all the ancient stories about the deaths of gods appeal, to something profound in the human spirit. But it appeals all the more strongly because we know that this story is centred on one who really lived and really died. At its centre is not simply a myth, a tale, a poetic expression of eternal truths, but a real act of communication which a man died to make.

Both the act of Jesus and the repeated story of Jesus are a statement of faith. To be a Christian is to join Jesus in that faith.

So far so rational. But is the faith justified? The church has always said emphatically, Yes! This is what the resurrection is all about. The resurrection is the proof that Jesus's faith *was* justified. Now here we are in difficulties. The resurrection cannot prove that Jesus' faith was justified unless we can be sure that it really happened. And the question of whether it did happen is a historical problem of the greatest complexity and delicacy. I am not prejudging the issue of the historicity of the resurrection. I am prepared to leave open the possibility that it did actually take place. But no one who has looked closely at the evidence could deny that as sober historians we must leave open the possibility that it did not. Now an event cannot prove anything if we cannot be certain that it ever took place. What the story of the resurrection does prove, of course, and prove abundantly, is that the earliest Christians themselves were thoroughly convinced that Jesus's faith was justified. *They* had no doubts whether the resurrection happened. In this respect our position is different from theirs. They had no reason to challenge the historicity of the resurrection, and in this sense they believed that they had a certain guarantee not only of the ultimate triumph of what Jesus stood for, but of his status as the Son of

God. But for us the resurrection itself is a matter for faith, and so we are again wholly in the realm of faith, as Jesus himself was. Indeed, it might be argued that the resurrection claim never was more than an attempt to bring forward into the here and now a certainty which properly belongs only to the last time. If we are to speak of the triumph of Christ we can do so only by faith.

We can, it is true, speak of the triumph of Christ in another sense. Jesus's love triumphed in that it remained true to itself. It was not defeated. Neither in life nor in death did Jesus compromise the values he stood for. We might again use the parallel of Martin Luther King to explain this. Martin Luther King's death was in a real sense no defeat. He had devoted himself to the cause of the civil rights movement and of non-violence. To kill him neither changed that devotion nor compromised his principles. If his opponents could have provoked him to violence, or frightened him into abandoning the struggle, that would have been real defeat. His assassination was, in a sense, a demonstration of their inability to defeat him. In a similar sense we can say that Jesus was undefeated. But this is not the same as saying that the way of Jesus must in the end be the right way, that on some cosmic scale or in some eternal dimension this way must be justified.

If we are to view the death of Jesus simply as an assertion of the values for which he stood, we can go no further than this. His death is an appeal to us to share his faith, an appeal for allegiance, an appeal to stand on his side. It is an assertion not that love triumphs, but that it deserves to. It is an assertion that if in the end love fails; if there is no resurrection and no God; if the mindless forces of the universe prove hostile at the last to the values we exalt, we should rather be wrong, with Christ, than right with the uncommitted. We should rather be wrong, not because it is more comforting, but because it is better.

This is not an attitude to be despised, though it falls short of the full Christian gospel as it has always been preached. Some may claim that in the present state of uncertainty it is as far as we can go. But even if we go only so far, we have salvaged an important fraction of what Christianity has always stood for. The attitude I have indicated may sound like one of despair and pessimism. It is not. It is the statement of an optimist, but of one who is prepared to face the possiblity that the pessimists may turn out to be right. To have faith does not mean to pretend to more certainty than the situation warrants. To believe means to look uncertainty in the face, and to go on living, if necessary to the bitter end, as if certain things were true, accepting the possiblility all the while that they *might* not be true.

Bringing God into it

But we are not obliged to stop there. Abelard himself did not stop there. For Abelard, the death of Christ is emphatically God's act, and this is part of the strength of his theory. If we can bring back God, if we can concede the possibility that God exists, then the possibility is immediately open that Jesus's death means something more than I have so far suggested. The life and death of Jesus might then be *God's* communication, *God's* statement. It is one thing to say that Jesus lived and died to communicate certain values, a certain way of looking at things. We can all see the appeal of these values and this point of view. Most of us would agree that it would be nice if Jesus's standpoint were justified and some of us might even go so far as to live as if it were. But if Jesus really was the Son of God, the Word of God, then this is quite another thing. For then we should have to say that the values he stood for, the way of looking at things which he tried to inculcate, are of eternal validity. They are no longer just the good ideas or the high principles of a man, or even of a whole community or tradition. They are ultimately the only principles by which human action should be judged.

As we saw, the declaration that Jesus rose from the dead does not dispense with the need for faith, for historically speaking we cannot be sure that the resurrection really took place. The resurrection is itself an object of faith. Similarly, the declaration that Jesus is the Son of God or the Word of God does not dispense with the necessity of faith, for we cannot be sure that God exists. God, too, is an object of faith. Perhaps when we say that Jesus is the Son of God or the Word we are doing no more than assert our belief in the eternal validity of what Jesus stands for.

The life and death of Jesus have an effect on us because they communicate with us. They affect our emotions, they affect our thinking, our way of looking at things. They have this effect in the way that story or drama always affect us, but to an infinitely higher degree. To watch well acted tragedy on the stage, to watch the tragedy of Oedipus or the slow death of Lear, is a harrowing experience. But to watch real tragedy, to see real death, is more so. When on Good Friday we hear for maybe the thousandth time the story of the passion read, it makes its impact not only because it hangs together dramatically, because it is the stuff of which high tragedy is made, because it echoes myths and uses images which pull at something in the atavistic depths of our souls (though all these statements about it are correct), but because we know it happened. And the impact is increased a millionfold as soon as we allow our imagination to play on the idea that Jesus might be what Christians have always claimed him to be. Let the cautious agnostic try an experiment. Let him listen to that story, and let him for a moment concede the possibility that it *might* be true.

For the Christian himself, the impact of the story is certainly dependent on his conviction that it *is* true. That is, not only did the crucifixion happen, but Jesus *is* the Son of God; what he said and what he stood for *are* eternally valid; and if the ubiquitous myths and legends of dying saviours and dying gods have any power, it is because they are foreshadowings of this one real event.

Let us for a moment come back once more to Abelard. His interpretation of the death of Christ is satisfying in that it offers an explanation of how that death affects us. We can see how death can be a form of communication. We can see how the death of Jesus could communicate forcibly the ideas which he

111

held. We may even see that, granted the existence of God, what Jesus communicates might be not his own truth but God's truth, eternally valid truth. We can see how the death of Christ can influence us by appealing both to the emotions and the mind. It can enlist us on Christ's side in the struggle, enable us to see the world from his point of view. Does it do more? Does the death of Christ only 'work' in so far as we respond to it? Is it *only* by appealing to our emotions and our will that it makes a difference to us? Until very recent times Christians have generally denied that explanations of the type offered by Abelard were entirely adequate, and Abelard himself would probably have agreed. As I said earlier, he seems to have thought of his own interpretation as an addition to the traditional ones, not an alternative to them.

To put this another way: I analysed the objects for which a man might voluntarily die into two sorts. A man might die in order to communicate something, or in order to achieve a specific end. So far we have thought of the death of Christ solely in terms of communication. Could it be seen as accomplishing anything else, anything more objective?

We can answer yes to this question only if we are prepared to bring back what I have called Christian mythology, if we are willing to talk as the traditional interpretations of the atonement do in terms of an objective transaction, or at least of an effect which the death of Christ has on God himself. The difference between the Abelardian theory and nearly all the earlier ones is that Abelard thinks of the death of Christ as having its effect on man, on ourselves, whereas the others mostly think of its effects as being primarily on God. On Abelard's interpretation the death of Christ does not change God's attitude to men or to men's sins. It demonstrates what that attitude has been all along. Theories such as those of Anselm, or the theory of penal substitution, so beloved of latter day Protestantism, envisage the death of Christ as changing the attitude of God.

What is called the patristic theory, an interpretation of the atonement which was widely subscribed to in the early Christian centuries, thinks of the work of Christ as having its effect not on God but on the devil. Christ rescued us, paid our ransom, delivering us from the devil's clutches. The fathers talk picturesquely of Christ either battling with the devil, or bargaining with him, or defeating him in a battle of wits, deceiving him by offering him a price for men's souls which the devil could not hold.

Are these interpretations saying anything valuable about the work of Christ which it would be a mistake to abandon? I believe that they are. If the work of Christ is genuinely God's act, then its validity cannot ultimately depend on human response to it. To put it another way: if the death of Christ is making some sort of statement, and if that statement is true, then it must still be true even if nobody believes it or responds to it. This is one of the things we mean when we talk about its eternal validity or describe it as God's act.

If someone writes a definitive work on a subject he has accomplished something. He has accomplished something real, substantial, objective. Even if no one should ever read what he has written, it is still there. It is there to be consulted. The information in it is there to be picked up. And the objectivity of the writer's achievement is beyond dispute, in spite of the fact that it does not become actual communication until someone is interested enough to read it. Christ's accomplishment is real and objective at least in this sense.

Having looked at the work of Christ, having seen his death as in some way a communication, or as an attempt to communicate, we must come back to the question, how does the life and death of Christ actually help me to live with guilt, or to live with all my other problems and dilemmas? Before I attempt an answer I want to insert a chapter in parenthesis.

NOTES

1. Lev. 5.5–13.
2. London: Jonathan Cape, 1961.
3. See pp. 24 f.
4. 'The Outcasts of Poker Flat', *Collected Works*, London: Chatto and Windus, 1890–1911, Vol. II.

5. See M. Eliade, *Myth and Reality*, London: George Allen and Unwin, 1964, pp. 99 ff.

6. See pp. 68 f.

7. Abelard himself seems to be developing a suggestion made earlier by Augustine in *De Catechizandis Rudibus*, 4, 7. See R. S. Franks, *A History of the Doctrine of the Work of Christ*, London: Hodder, n.d. Vol. 1, p. 134.

8. He did reject the idea of redemption from the devil, but in this he was not alone among mediaeval theologians. He is critical of the notion of a ransom paid to God, but does hold that the death of Christ in some direct fashion procures the forgiveness of sins. And Abelard is capable of expounding the death of Christ in quite traditional terms.

7   Analogies?

In an earlier chapter I expressed a certain impatience with the analogies which have been used to explain the work of Christ, but suggested that, if we must resort to analogies, then possibly some could be found which would do duty in the twentieth century.[1] What I am going to do now is to make two suggestions, one of which is certainly an analogy. About the second I am not so sure.

The Redeemer

The idea of the divine redeemer or rescuer is a very ancient one. Saviour gods were familiar figures to mankind long before Christ was ever cast in that role. The background to the idea of the divine redeemer is one I have already sketched in Chapter 3.[2] Man has always felt himself, at least from time to time, under pressure. In ancient times he expressed this feeling by talking about the superhuman powers which held him, and his world, in bondage. Today we talk in other terms, but ancient and modern men agree in this, that whatever name we give to the powers that hold us, they are certainly too much for us. We cannot by our own strength throw them off. They have got a hold inside us, sabotaging our efforts from within. It was feelings of this sort that prompted the well-nigh universal belief in, or hope for, a saviour. This saviour is always himself super-human, either divine or at least semi-divine. He has to be. A man who was no more than a man would be dominated like the rest of us. Mankind has always felt that the saviour, if he is to succeed, must be able to call on more than human power.

This feeling that we are being conspired against, that things are ganging up on us, that therefore we are defeated before we

115

start, that 'we can't win', seems to me to be as alive as ever it was in the ancient world. To present Christ against this background should therefore have a strong appeal to the imagination, though to be sure, it provides us with no rational explanation of how it is that Christ helps us. It is *only* an analogy and suffers from the drawbacks of analogies. It can only be really helpful to those who are able to concede that there is an objectivity to the work of Christ. If Christ has done something which actually alters man's status in the world, if he has accomplished something which has an objective effect on man's predicament, then the analogy affords us a kind of illustration of what he has done. Or if a man has an unmistakable experience of salvation; if he knows at first hand the relief that faith can bring, then the analogy can assist him to put that experience into words.

The modern word for a redeemer is the ombudsman. The ombudsman is the one who to some extent stands outside the system. When the system itself provides no machinery for appeal against its decisions, or when a man feels wronged by the very machinery which society has set up to safeguard his rights, when the mindless bureaucrats have sent their final cyclostyled refusal to consider his case, it is to the ombudsman that he appeals. In modern life we are all of us familiar with the need for this kind of saviour. When our letter to the managing director himself is passed back by his secretary for reply to the very department about which we were complaining; when the salesman points out that in signing the guarantee we signed away our rights at common law; when the man in the complaints department draws our attention to the clause in which the company disclaims all liability for whatever loss it happens to be that we have suffered, the ombudsman is what we need. We need someone from outside the system, someone who does not belong to the organization, someone who is not himself caught up in the machine and dependent on the machine for his promotion, who can *make* them listen to our complaint, *force* them to give us justice.

The ombudsman is the one who intervenes at the moment when we are overpowered, who comes to our aid at the point

116

where things are just too much for us. The ombudsman is the one who is on our side when no one else is, to whom we can turn when there is no one else to turn to. There are those who will bear testimony that this is what Christ does for them, though again I insist that this is no explanation of how exactly he does it. This woman will witness that Christ restored sanity seconds before she murdered the kids and put her head in the oven; this man that Christ restored courtesy minutes before the unseemly quarrel with his colleague, or before he threw the ledger at the boss's head; another that Christ restored love, or at least pity, an hour before he walked out on his wife.

As an *explanation*, the analogy of the ombudsman redeemer is a non-starter, but as a description of some Christians' experience it is not without merit.

The healer

It has long seemed astonishing to me that when Christians were looking for analogies by which to explain or expound the work of Christ, they virtually ignored the one which in the New Testament is the most prominent of all. They framed their doctrine of the atonement in terms of institutions, ideas, beliefs which were subscribed to by the men of western Europe or of the Mediterranean lands, and then only for a few generations, and they left on one side an analogy which is within the common experience of mankind.

In the gospels Christ is presented throughout as the healer. And this healing is not regarded as an accidental feature of his work; it is not even an essential accompaniment to the work. It *is* the work. What Jesus does for people's bodies is part and parcel of what he does for their souls. This is the assumption of the gospel writers. The Aramaic language, which was Jesus's vernacular, has a verb which might most literally be rendered 'to revive', 'to restore life', 'to give life' or 'to make alive'. But it also means 'to heal', and it also means 'to save'. To read the ancient Syriac version of the gospels (Syriac being simply an Aramaic dialect) is a most curious experience, because where our familiar gospels have different words and expressions, and speak of healing, saving or giving life, the Syriac only has one. It is always the same word, for what looks to us like all these different activities. I am not suggesting that Jesus and the disciples and all the other people who spoke this language could not see the difference between these various activities, but it does look as if they saw a ready connexion between them which we are disinclined to see. To the first Christians there is no doubt that the healing work of Jesus was not merely a kind of parable of his atoning work (though it *was* that), but an actual demonstration of it. When Jesus asked: 'Which is easier, to say, "Your sins are forgiven", or to say, "Rise, take up your bed and walk"?'[3] he seems to be suggesting that whether he talks in terms of healing or of forgiving is a matter of indifference, that they are just different ways of saying the same thing.

Our own experience confirms that in many contexts this is true. To remove our tensions, to help us get rid of our sense of guilt, to enable us to face life and to cope with its difficulties, to give us back our confidence and our self-respect – what would the process be called, supposing it could be done? Healing, forgiveness, salvation? Any of these would be at least half appropriate.

No, after all I do not think it is an analogy. If Christ can help with such problems, if he can give any aid to oppressed man, man convinced of his sin, man under pressure, then this is not an activity which is *like* healing. It is healing.

So we return to our question: can Christ do this? Does Christianity help us to live with guilt and with our other infirmities? And if so, how?

NOTES

1. See p. 69.
2. See especially pp. 54 ff.
3. Mark 3.9.

8 Community and Communication

The two most awkward-looking questions which we have so far encountered in this book are: can we say that the work of Christ achieved anything objective, i.e. anything apart from its effects on my mind and my emotions? And second (maybe this is a different form of the same question), how can the work of Christ after two thousand years have an effect on *me*? How can it help me to overcome *my* deficiencies and to live with *my* guilt?

Perhaps it is only those of us who have been brainwashed by four centuries or so of Protestantism who find the questions so intolerably difficult. Your brainwashed Protestant (I can afford to be rude, I am a member of the species) stumbles most seriously over these questions because he tends to look in the wrong direction for the answers. He tends to think in terms of some quite direct and mystical link between the work of his Saviour and his own soul. Much of the imagery which Christians have resorted to down the ages suggests such a direct and mystical link, some tangible experience in which the soul is washed in the blood of the lamb, or reborn or enlightened. Now I do not want to go so far as to suggest that no direct and mystical link exists. But if it does, it seems to be possible to talk about it only in the language of poetry. When we try to pin down in rational terms just what the link is between Christ and my soul it is very difficult to do.

Nevertheless, there is another direction in which we can look. There is a way in which we can give an objective account of how Christ affects us and point to an objective achievement of his life and death. The life and death of Jesus created the church. This is not only an objective but a very concrete achievement; and however else Christ may have affected me, he has certainly affected me through his church in a very objective and easily understood fashion.

If we are looking at the death of Christ as a communication, then the church is the community of those who have heard that communication and, in a measure, responded to it. It is the community of those whose perspective has been changed by Christ, or ostensibly so. It is the community of those who are willing, or who like to think they are willing, or who would genuinely like to be willing, to see things, the world, and themselves, from the Christ point of view.

One has to put in all these reservations because it goes without saying that the church, from one point of view, is a colossal failure. It preaches a gospel which few, if any, of its members manage to live up to. Its 'public image', even in the eyes of those who belong to it, is very poor. This is why one hesitates to point to the church as the effective, the tangible link between Christ two thousand years ago and the believer now. It is such an unattractive link. But my point is that it is a real and perceptible link, and indeed a very effective one.

In fact the church is not only the body of those who heard and who have responded to the communication. It is the only body which preserves and passes on the communication, but it actually exercises a great deal of control over the communication itself. It does not merely pass it on, but interprets it, tries to show what it means and how it applies in the contemporary situation.

And how does it do this? It preaches the gospel. It tells the story. It celebrates the sacraments. I have said enough, I hope, about the power of story and of drama and of how they have their effect upon us. And this effect is multiplied a millionfold when they are heard or participated in within the living community of believers. In the end the story and the drama speak for themselves, and speak better than any of us can speak for them. One may watch a passion play at one's local church, badly produced and badly acted, and knowing from personal acquaintance that some of the people who take part are not actually very pleasant characters, and yet find it moving. Why? Because here is something greater than the church. Here is a story of which the church is not worthy and by which the church itself is judged. And we in the church do not deny this. We are not presenting ourselves. We have no illusions about ourselves. We know we are not very nice people. We are presenting Christ. We are telling the story, enacting the drama. It can speak for itself. All our proffered explanations of it are really made only for our own intellectual satisfaction. If you have not felt the pull of the story you will find them incomprehensible. And if you have, they will be superfluous.

Forget the interpretations of the atonement. Come to communion on Maundy Thursday. Join there with your fellows, believers and half-believers. Listen to the gospel. Say the words with us. Take the bread and take the wine, and find in that converting ordinance what all the explanations can not convey.

I have long felt that there is too much of a gap between our theological talk and our sacramental experience. We have developed a theology *of* the sacraments, of course, but we have not really produced a sacramental theology. I have no right to speak for denominations other than my own, though I suspect that what is true of my own Methodism is perhaps equally true of other branches of Protestantism. We have paid lip service to the importance of the sacraments, and have even gone so far, sometimes, as to give them an important place in our practice, but we have never given them an important place in our *thinking*. We have worked out our doctrine of the atonement almost without reference to our doctrine of the sacraments, with the consequent impoverishment of both. We have called men to repentance from their sins without going far out of our way to tell them that this might have something to do with their baptism, and without often relating the invitation to repentance to the invitation to the Lord's table. Yet the atonement can only make sense to a man when Christ is real to him. And where can Christ be made more real to him than in the sacraments?

The church is the community in which Christ can become real. He can become real in the sacraments and in the worship of the church. He can become real in the life of the church. I have earlier argued that a man can live with his guilt and his failure when he

121

learns to forgive himself, when he can accept his guilt and failure as facts, and accept himself in spite of them. I have said that Christ can help him, in that Christ is the one who knows all and is prepared to forgive all. But this only works if Christ can be made real to the guilty one. The church can make both Christ and his forgiveness real, by being an accepting community.

Those of us who belong to the church are highly conscious of its shortcomings (much more so than are the people outside it). Many of us can be fiercely critical of the church. But to the church's credit it must be said that for very many people the church is precisely what I have described, a community where they are accepted as they are accepted nowhere else. Of course, the church does not always succeed in this, but it succeeds oftener than even some of its supporters would imagine. If, as is often said, the church is three-quarters full of oddities who do not fit in anywhere else, I for one regard this as something to be proud of.

To be a Christian is to belong to the church. It is to stand within a particular community with a particular perspective, within a particular tradition. In practice, for the majority of us, this belonging to a community looms far larger in our religious life than the precise content of Christian belief. Anyone who has ever listened to a group of ordinary church members trying to talk about Christianity can bear witness that remarkably few of them know what Christians are even supposed to believe. Even fewer can express Christian beliefs in an articulate way, and fewer still could rationally defend them. What on earth makes these people go to church at all? It is easy to probe into their reasons and to decide that most of them are bad ones. But what most of the reasons come down to is that the church is a community in which, however discontented we may sometimes be with it, we feel we belong. I am not sure that, put in this way, it is such a bad reason after all. For most of us, faith is belonging.

The word 'church', of course, conjures up all kinds of pictures, and some of them are bound to be misleading. I have perhaps made it sound as if the church is an intimate, deeply spiritual community. We all know it is not. My local church, on any average Sunday evening, consists of a congregation of, say, a hundred and fifty. I have no profound and intimate relationship with all of the other one hundred and forty-nine. Some of them I do not even know by name. For me the *effective* church is much smaller. The community of people who actually affect my Christian outlook and experience, from whom I actually learn anything about the spiritual life, is much smaller. Some of them I only know because I have read their books; they are not personal acquaintances at all. Some of them I have not met or written to for years, but their influence is indelible. Now that I come to think of it, some of those who not only affected but still do affect my Christian life most strongly are dead. Perhaps, on second thoughts, the effective church for me is not so small after all. But all of them, present or absent, on earth or in heaven, are part of the community which makes Christ real to me, the community in which I find it possible to look at myself and my guilt and my failures and my dilemmas in a certain light, and therefore to go on living with myself.

For Further Reading

F. R. Barry, *The Atonement*, Hodder & Stoughton 1958
F. W. Dillistone, *The Christian Understanding of the Atonement*, James Nisbet 1968
Mircea Eliade, *Myth and Reality*, Allen & Unwin 1964
H. A. Hodges, *The Pattern of Atonement*, SCM Press 1955
L. Hodgson, *The Doctrine of the Atonement*, James Nisbet 1951
John Knox, *The Death of Christ*, Collins 1967
G. W. H. Lampe, *Reconciliation in Christ*, Longmans, Green & Co. 1955
J. G. MacKenzie, *Guilt*, Allen & Unwin 1962

SCM BOOK CLUB

SCM Press Ltd · 56 Bloomsbury Street · London WC1B 3QX

Editor's Letter

I was going through some files last week, and came across my first correspondence over the study project four years ago, with David Edwards, my predecessor (now Rector of St Margaret's, Westminster), and David Jenkins (now at the World Council of Churches in Geneva). It seems only yesterday that we were discussing what to do, and holding a conference to collect a variety of ideas, and now here already is the last book in the series.

I went on to look at some of the letters that you wrote as the books began to come out: 'too difficult', 'is destroying my faith', 'marvellous', 'the best thing that has come out of the Club', 'useless'. Almost every shade of opinion is represented, from one side to the other. Some people have left the Club as a result; others have nobly continued, although they are doubtful about the project; many new members have joined.

Has it been worth it? I don't know what you think. But I do know that in their more expensive dress, as *centrebooks,* sold to the public, the volumes in the study project series have sold better than any other group of books we've published, and the name '*centrebooks*' has become a real landmark. I'm most grateful to all the authors for producing such splendid writing and to all of you for making it possible by your membership; and while comparisons are invidious, I'm not sure that we haven't got the best book of them all to finish with.

The same files also contained your first reactions to the new series of biographies which begin in November: 'Not simple biographies after what we've enjoyed over the past year!', wrote one correspondent. I wonder what you'll think when they actually come. I've read the first two in typescript and very much enjoyed them. I hope you do too. In any case, write and tell me your views.

John Bowden

LIVING WITH GUILT

A Review by Alan Richardson

Alan Richardson is Dean of York and Chairman of the Board of Directors of SCM Press.

I am a quick reader. I have to be, because there is so much that must be read – not only theological writing but documents of all kinds, from committee reports to engineers' appraisals of the structural repairs of York Minster. But when I started on Henry McKeating's *Living with Guilt* I found that I could not read it at my quick rate. This was not because it was hard-going or obscure. It is remarkably lucid and its English style is much more 'contemporary' than that of the *New English Bible*. It is written throughout in the language which we speak everyday and it contains no jargon at all; it deals with the profoundest human issues without resorting to the esoteric vocabulary with which so many sociologists, psychologists and theologians deface and obscure their pages. I found that I wanted to read it thoughtfully, because it immediately became obvious that it was worth reading that way.

The book deals with the problems and frustrations which ordinary people experience every day in language which they might themselves use, if only they had thought about them as deeply as the author has done. Which of the feelings of guilt that we all have are irrational, but nevertheless refuse to go away, and which of them are rationally grounded in moral convictions? How are they to be dealt with in either case? To be human is to live with guilt – not only our personal guilt but that of the society of which we are members. Mr McKeating illustrates from modern novels and plays the truth that guilt is not an invention of Christianity but is recognized as a condition of human existence by perceptive people in every age, including our own.

Can anything be done about it? Most theological answers, which have been inherited from the past, do not seem persuasive to us today. In any case the problem is not only a theological one but a human one, and humanistic psychologists and sociologists have a lot to say about it. Nor is it a merely theoretical problem, for it follows us around like our own shadow. Even if we are sincere Christian believers, we still have to live with it; we cannot escape from our shadow. How do the resources of everyday Christian living and believing help us to understand our predicament and so to be more 'adequate' persons?

I welcome this book as a new start in theology, though its author does not claim to be a theologian at all – merely an Old Testament scholar. What he is offering us is what we most need, a theology of common sense, or a theology of everyday experience. Amongst the curious varieties of slogans we have recently been offered is the one which declares that theology is anthropology, that is, merely a way of talking about man in religious language. The truth is that talking sensibly about the human condition is the most convincing way of showing that the doctrine of God is relevant to us today. This book does just that.

3

THIS MONTH'S AUTHOR

Henry McKeating

Dr McKeating writes: 'I was born during the great depression and brought up during the war on the West Cumberland coalfield. My relations (there are scores of them) were all miners, Methodists and socialists, not necessarily in that order; the articulate working class, in fact. (There *is* an articulate working class, though the sociologists don't seem to have noticed.)

'I was educated at the local grammar school, entered the Methodist ministry and trained at Handsworth College, Birmingham. I acquired three external London degrees, BD, MTh and PhD (much later), and had a year's ecumenical exposure in Strasbourg, where I learnt more from the Jews and Catholics than from the Protestants. Apart from that I never went to university. I'm still trying to decide whether this is an advantage or a disadvantage.

'I served briefly in two country circuits in Norfolk: Thetford, which was nice, and Hunstanton, which was nasty. In desperation I sought shelter in academic life, but found human nature much the same. I've lectured in the Department of Theology at Nottingham University for the last eleven years, but have written nothing worthy of note. Ostensibly I'm an Old Testament scholar. My hobbies are bringing up a family of four and a little gentle mountaineering.'

Printed in Great Britain by Billing & Sons Ltd., Guildford and London